The One Minute Negotiator

Simple Steps to Reach Better Agreements

Don Hutson
George Lucas

EasyRead Large

Copyright Page from the Original Book

The One Minute Negotiator

Berrett-Koehler Publishers, Inc.
235 Montgomery Street, Suite 650
San Francisco, California 94104-2916
Tel: (415) 288-0260, Fax: (415) 362-2512
www.bkconnection.com

Ordering information for print editions
Quantity sales. Special discounts are available on quantity purchases by corporations, associations, and others. For details, contact the "Special Sales Department" at the Berrett-Koehler address above.
Individual sales. Berrett-Koehler publications are available through most bookstores. They can also be ordered directly from Berrett-Koehler: Tel: (800) 929-2929; Fax: (802) 864-7626; www.bkconnection.com
Orders for college textbook/course adoption use. Please contact Berrett-Koehler: Tel: (800) 929-2929; Fax: (802) 864-7626.
Orders by U.S. trade bookstores and wholesalers. Please contact Ingram Publisher Services, Tel: (800) 509-4887; Fax: (800) 838-1149; E-mail: customer.service@ingrampublisherservices.com; or visit www.ingram publisherservices.com/Ordering for details about electronic ordering.

Berrett-Koehler and the BK logo are registered trademarks of Berrett-Koehler Publishers, Inc.

First Edition
Hardcover print edition ISBN 978-1-60509-586-8
PDF e-book ISBN 978-1-60509-620-9
IDPF e-book ISBN 978-1-60509-621-6

2010-2

Production Management: Michael Bass Associates
Cover Design: Richard Adelson

TABLE OF CONTENTS

More Praise for The One Minute Negotiator

"The marketplace is crying out for better negotiation skills and this book provides them! Great story, great skills, great takeaways—don't miss this one."
—Bill Bartmann, NASDAQ/ *USA Today* /Ernst & Young National Entrepreneur of the Year and author of *Bailout Riches*

"Finally, a book that recognizes you can't negotiate the same way with different personalities! It's not just a techniques book but a strategy book for matching the appropriate techniques to the uniquenesses of all parties—a very content-rich book!"
—Don Thoren, President, Thoren Consulting Group

"A simple and straightforward yet elegant and compelling 'negotiation parable.' Even an experienced negotiator, such as I believed myself to be, was instantly awakened to new and better techniques and strategies. I excitedly anticipate that *The One Minute Negotiator* will bring me even better results!"
—Dr. Larry Markson, author of *Talking to Yourself Is NOT Crazy*

"I've been an entrepreneur in Canada for almost forty years. You never stop learning, you never stop growing, you never stop expanding, and it's always exciting. If you want to add to your knowledge and future success, then you need to read Don Hutson's and George Lucas's new book, *The One Minute Negotiator.*"

—Dr. Peter Legge, OBC, LLD (Hon.), CSP, CPAE, Chairman/CEO/Publisher, Canada Wide Media Limited

"Don Hutson and George Lucas have taken the art of negotiating, cut it up into bite-size pieces, blended it into an entertaining story, and given us a brand-new perspective on negotiating. I think this must read book will be yet another bestseller for Don and George."

—L.D. Beard, cofounder and former CEO, Medtronic Sofamor Danek

"Don and George tell an engaging story with concepts that equip the negotiator within all of us with the needed resources to transform us from 'negotiaphobics' into 'negotiaphenoms'!"

—Burton Goldfield, President and CEO, TriNet

"This book and the concept of negotiaphobia wowed me! After reading it I feel I have the tools to be a better negotiator than ever. Don't miss this one—it is a read that will alter your skills forever!"

—Allen J. Pathmarajah, Executive Chairman, AJP Advisers Group, Singapore

"This is simply a great read that I wish would have been available much earlier in my career. I have negotiated billions of dollars' worth of transactions, and I'm confident that the level of success would have been significantly enhanced through the learning offered in *The One Minute Negotiator!"*

—Jerry Britton, Group President, Textron Financial Corporation

"This book took me directly to the heart and soul of negotiating, and it spoke to me personally. It is for anybody who wants to personally and professionally negotiate with greater expertise. This is a must-read and must-implement book!"

—Jim Fite, President, Century 21 Judge Fite Company

"Hutson and Lucas have written an exciting book that is really needed! Businesspeople today struggle mightily with how to protect margin and negotiate price, and they need simple yet successful strategies. *The One Minute Negotiator* is the ticket. Don't miss this book or it will cost you dearly!"

—Tom Hudak, President, Akron Brass

"If you fear or even have a slight hesitance toward negotiating, this book is a must-read. It is well written in a story format and loaded with practical win/win negotiation skills and strategies."

—Dr. Tony Alessandra, coauthor of *The Platinum Rule* and author of *Charisma*

"This book is a masterpiece on the science of negotiation and the art of relational capital. Read it to learn. Study it to succeed."

—Dr. Nido Qubein, President, High Point University, and Chairman, Great Harvest Bread Company

"Effective negotiation occurs only after thorough preparation. *The One Minute Negotiator* is a great tool to use in that preparation."

—R. Brad Martin, former Chairman and CEO, Saks Incorporated

" *The One Minute Negotiator* simply makes sense. In our international environment we need a system that is transferable in multiple countries, and this book provides it! It teaches the benefits of balancing both the relationships and tactics to achieve best results!"

—Adam Wood, Sales and Marketing Director, Sonoco-Alcore, Brussels, Belgium

"This simple 'One Minute' process cures a disease that affects both our professional and personal lives. The benefits of the three-step process and it's reach will be immeasurable!"

—Jorge A. Rojas, Manager of Operations, Alimer S.A., San Jose, Costa Rica

"This fast-paced book on negotiating is a must-read for any businessperson. I highly recommend it. Don Hutson has received universally high marks as a resource to our company, and the skills we will gain from *The One Minute Negotiator* will add measurably to our retailers' success!"

—Jeffrey R. Fausett, President and CEO, Aquatech Pools

"The content in *The One Minute Negotiator* is a great solution to a problem countless business professionals have had for decades!"

—Jack Soden, CEO, Elvis Presley Enterprises

"Enlightening! Embedded in this readable business fable are practical tools to assess your style and learn how to negotiate better with others despite their differences. These insights will make you a more effective and successful negotiator!"

—Mark Sanborn, CSP, CPAE, President, Sanborn & Associates, Inc.

"*The One Minute Negotiator* delivers a clear and actionable process that is useful and timely. The matrix on negotiation styles is an excellent framework for both organizations and individuals."

—Frederick F. Avery, former President, Kraft Food Ingredients

"In the NFL, negotiating calls is not an option. But off the field we are challenged daily with negotiation encounters. This book will teach you new skills and get you better results!"

—Jim Tunney, former NFL referee, Super Bowls VI, XI, and XII

OTHER BOOKS BY THE AUTHORS

Don Hutson

The Sale

Insights into Excellence (with the members of Speakers Roundtable)
The Winning Spirit (anthology)
Inspiring Others to Win (anthology)
Speaking Secrets of the Masters (with the members of Speakers Roundtable)
Time Management Is an Oxymoron (with Maynard Rolston)
The Contented Achiever (with George Lucas and Chris Crouch)
Selling with Style (with Tony Alessandra and Scott Zimmerman)
Taking Charge: Lessons in Leadership (anthology)
Conversations on Service and Sales (anthology)
The One Minute Entrepreneur (with Ken Blanchard and Ethan Willis)

George Lucas

Marketing Strategies (with O.C. Ferrell, David Luck and Michael D. Hartline)
The Contented Achiever (with Don Hutson and Chris Crouch)

Retailing (with Robert Bush and Larry Gresham)
Inspiring Others to Win (anthology)

Dedication

We dedicate this book to our loving children:

Don's: *Sandy, Scott, and Kevin*
George's: *Taylor and Austin*

They have brought us much joy, and we love them for that. They have also taught us a lot, and we thank them for that.

But most of all we love each of you for just being yourselves.

Foreword

When people think about negotiation, they tend to think about win-lose—in other words, somebody's going to win, and somebody's going to lose. Many people go so far as to associate negotiation with the ability to "get them before they get you." That's not what *The One Minute Negotiator* is all about. One of the key messages from this book is that you can complete a negotiation without victimizing others—or becoming a victim—in the process. Rather than fighting over a finite pie, you can use the skills taught in this book to actually create a bigger pie.

Maybe you don't think you need negotiating skills. Many of us believe we can glad-hand our way through any relationship; we trust that our good intentions will create good outcomes. While collaboration is a noble goal, if you're negotiating with a tough, competitive individual who has no interest in collaborating, you might as well be standing on the railroad tracks trying to negotiate with a speeding train. You need to be able to recognize what you're dealing with early on and use a strategy that works with that type of person. This book will teach you how to see the train coming and get on board, rather than getting flattened by it.

The One Minute Negotiator also will introduce you to the Negotiation Matrix, a tool that will help you recognize the four negotiation strategies: avoidance, accommodation, competition, and collaboration. The ability to diagnose a person's negotiating strategy will help you get the results you want and at the same time enhance your relationships. Once you have internalized this skill, it will pay you dividends forever. You will be able to listen more skillfully, evaluate others more accurately, discern people's goals, and strategize for the best possible outcomes.

So don't be "negotiaphobic." Read this book and enjoy the ride to greater collaboration and success.

—Dr. Ken Blanchard, coauthor of *The One Minute Manager*® and *The One Minute Entrepreneur*™

CHAPTER 1

I Have Negotiaphobia?!

Two Tickets for Paradise

The sign in Terminal H of Miami International Airport proclaimed, "Welcome to Miami." As Jay Baxter read this message and then looked for the arrow directing him to baggage claim, he doubted that he had ever felt more welcome anytime and anyplace in his life. He and his wife, Laura, had won a spot on the Top Producers Award Trip his company held annually for all salespeople who exceeded their sales quota by more than 10 percent during the prior year.

That company, XL Information Solutions, had considered canceling the trip this year in an effort to reduce costs. The organization's president stepped in at the last minute and saved the event with the idea of making it not only a reward but also a relevant educational experience. The president's memo mentioned getting a return on the investment, but everyone knew changes in tax laws restricting a company's ability to write off such excursions played a major role in the repositioning. Jay was glad the possibility of a cancellation had never leaked to his wife, Laura. She had been counting on this trip for six months, and it was the one legitimate explanation he could give her for all those late dinners and missed family events he had delivered to those he loved so much over the past year.

When they left Cleveland, it had been snowing and a chilling 21 degrees. Upon landing, the pilot told them it was 78 in Miami, and the passengers did not need to be told they were finally in "The Sunshine State." This was to be a glorious trip for the two of them. Laura's parents had come in from Chicago to watch their two teenagers, so they were on the verge of a trip without a care.

Not only had Jay qualified for this event, but his revenue total was the highest percentage over quota of all seventeen people who had earned the cruise. Many of his colleagues had e-mailed him indicating they felt he had a lock on the coveted "Salesperson of the Year" award. He already had a place of honor picked out to display the golden statue award, as well as the talking points for his acceptance speech.

Laura had heard the award was a possibility from several of the spouses, and on the flight down she mentioned using the additional bonus money as a down payment on a new home. He had put her off on this major change for some time, but as their negotiations continued, he was beginning to run out of excuses. One additional possibility Laura had not heard about—and Jay did nothing to get her hopes up on the issue—was that Jay would also be getting a promotion to the now-vacant regional sales manager position for the Upper Midwest. This accomplishment would not only make a higher monthly mortgage payment feasible but would also fulfill his career-long dream. He had coveted this position for years, and since the present manager announced his retirement several weeks ago, he had even found opportunities to sneak into this office space to have a look around.

"Laura, do you think I have a fear of negotiating?" Jay asked his wife as they walked through the terminal. She responded with her own question: "Why do you ask, dear?" He justified his question by informing her of the focus of the workshop that would be consuming much of his time on this trip. "This Dr. Pat guy's seminar program is called 'Treating Your Negotiaphobia.' In the description, he claims that even the most senior business professionals suffer from a disease that has its roots in the fear of negotiating, both in the workplace and in our personal life: *negotiaphobia.* I don't have that fear, do I?" Laura couldn't resist the opportunity to take a free shot or two at teasing her husband. "Well, Jay, you have plumbingphobia, as the faucet in the upstairs bathroom still drips. You have gardeningphobia given the weeds that are still in the flower beds from last summer. Given those fears, you may have negotiaphobia as well." Jay smirked and said, "Thanks, lover. Glad to always have your unconditional support."

When they reached baggage claim, their luggage was three of the first ten bags on the belt. Jay disliked checking luggage, but this time it worked like a charm. Ten minutes later, they were in the shuttle headed down I-95 to the Port of Miami. Departing the van at the pier, he tipped the shuttle driver, who when questioned repeatedly assured both of them that these bags would be in their stateroom in plenty of time to dress for dinner. "We have a simple process in place that works thousands of times each day," the driver confidently stated. They would just need to check in, set up credit for their incidental expenses, provide their passports, get on board, and start having fun.

The moment they stepped onto that massive ship they were engulfed in an atmosphere of festivity. Signing the $22 check for their welcome beverages, Jay instantly realized it would not take long to spend the $400 ship credit his company provided each couple on this three-night/four-day cruise to the Bahamas and then down to Key West. "Oh, well," he said to Laura, "this is not a time to worry about money; this is a time to celebrate, have fun, live graciously, and look toward what will most certainly be the future we have both worked so hard to achieve."

Ruinous Rumors

After the mandatory lifeboat drill, which was half serious (the crew) and half a joke and party time (the passengers), Jay and Laura went back to their cabin. It was cozy, but at least it had a small balcony to step out on and raise a toast to the poor souls who were not fortunate enough to be sailing off to sun and fun. Laura told Jay to shower first and then get out of there so she could get ready in peace and quiet. He dutifully obeyed.

Eduardo Carlos, XL's sales rep for the south Florida territory, had told Jay at the drill he wanted to talk with him. A dozen years ago, Jay and Eduardo had experienced the company's new employee orientation program together. They often bounced ideas off one another and considered themselves the two best players in the company at deciphering any new policy or finding the easy money in the annual changes in the compensation plan.

Jay put on his new pink and green flamingo and palm tree shirt he had brought along to a mixture of complaints and laughter from Laura, gave her a quick kiss, and headed off to find his friend.

Jay met Eduardo at the elevator midship on the Lido deck. They found a fairly quiet table to sit down at for their chat. "Jay, you are really doing one heck of a job keeping on a happy face given what's happening," Eduardo said.

"What are you talking about?" Jay asked. "We just wrapped up a fine year in a tough market, we are on a fantastic cruise ship, and I don't want to assume too much, but my Salesperson of the Year acceptance speech has a couple of really good one-liners in it. All better than that lead sled dog stuff Robert made us suffer through last year. Want to hear 'em?"

Eduardo looked shocked. "You really don't know, do you?"

"Know what?" was all Jay could say. He was wondering if someone had been fired or, worse yet, someone in the company might be seriously ill.

"I really hope you get a chance to use that speech next year. The rumor mill has Cathy Simmons getting the big prize at the awards banquet tonight," Eduardo cautiously told his friend.

"Cathy Simmons?" Jay said her name like he was talking about a plague. He was a good 8 percent ahead of her the last time he looked at XL's sales results. "This simply can't be true. I never even considered her serious competition." His voice trailed off as he spoke.

Eduardo went on, "There is no doubt that this is felony theft, my friend. You had one heck of a year. Word is that it was a real bloodbath at the executive committee meeting. Everyone thought you had it locked up, and then Bob Blankenship came in and turned everything upside down. I guess you can do that when you're the president of the company." The criteria for Salesperson of the Year award had always been a little vague, but tradition had it that the individual with the highest percentage above sales quota got the golden statue. Eduardo continued, "Blankenship comes in and says that given the pressure on profitability, gross margin had to be the primary criterion this year. After two more hours of aggressive politicking from all sides, Cathy came out on top."

Jay thought back to the year-end spreadsheet he had studied a few weeks ago and seemed to recall her being about 5 percent ahead of him in the contribution to company profit column. He did not think much about this at the time. He always thought Monte Beal, the New York rep, was his only serious competition. "Eduardo, how certain are you about this?"

"Man, do you think I'd be telling you this if it was not a done deal?" Eduardo seemed to have his sources pretty much everywhere, and the historical accuracy of his information only added to Jay's growing feeling of both panic and anger. "Jay, I hate to be the delivery man for bad news, but while we are putting it all on the table, you might as well know she likely will also be announced as the new regional sales manager for the Midwest. Apparently she went to some negotiation skills workshop about a year ago. An ex-college prof, a Dr. Pat Something, ran it. Get this: he is on this cruise and for the next couple of days will be conducting his workshop on board for all of us unfortunate souls. Can you believe it? My Luciana and your Laura get to hit the shore excursions with the spouse program, and we end up being cooped up in some dark meeting room with this egghead." Jay, still in shock, could only grimace and nod in agreement.

Jay slowly replied, "Can you believe this guy has actually come up with some disease we all apparently have? Something called—get this—negotiaphobia. Cathy Simmons really has Blankenship in her corner, doesn't she?"

Eduardo was clearly in agreement. "Hey, Jay, I hate hitting you with this all at once. I really assumed you knew. My friend, don't lose sight of the year you had. It was top-shelf, and things are going to work out for you. We are both survivors. Were that not the case, neither of us would have lasted a dozen years in this crazy business. You going to be okay?"

Jay assured him that he was fine, or at least he would be. With that, Eduardo said he had to check on one of Luciana's missing bags and then head back to their cabin to pick her up. "We'll look for you and Laura at the dinner. Maybe we can grab a table if they don't have assigned seating." With that, he was gone, and so was Jay's upbeat mood—every last ounce of it.

The Chance Encounter

Jay gave a glance at his watch and saw that he had fifteen more minutes before heading back for Laura. He went into the Beach Shack Lounge and ordered a beverage. As it arrived, he noticed some-one sliding onto the bar stool next to him, but he clearly was in no mood to chat.

"Where ya from?" he heard the guy ask.

"Cleveland."

"Darn nice city. I enjoy going there, though not necessarily during the winter."

Okay, Jay thought. That comment was positive enough to deserve the same question back. "What about you?"

"Well, I am sort of from everywhere these days, but I still consider San Angelo, Texas, home," the stranger said with the strong accent natives of that state are known for.

Jay looked down at the guy's shoes and his expectations were fulfilled. "Well, the cowboy boots are a dead giveaway. I should have known."

"I've got to ask you. Here we are on this cruise, and you look like your prize bull just died. What's got you down? Are you with that XL group running all over the boat?"

"Yeah, I am. Been with them about a dozen years," Jay said with absolutely zero emotion.

The stranger said, "Isn't this supposed to be a reward trip? You should be in a celebratory mood, man."

Jay told the Texan that he should have seen him an hour ago. "I *was* on cloud nine. I had my best sales year ever, with total confidence that it will be more of the same this year. Nearly all of my customers stayed with us, and I also managed to add enough new ones to have the highest percentage revenue above quota of anyone in the company. I won this trip for my wife and me, and thought I was a cinch for salesperson of the year." Jay was not certain why he was confiding in this stranger, but he went on. "I was in line for a big promotion as well. Now I hear from my best friend in the company that all of that was stolen from me by the woman who is our rep in St. Louis." The stranger nodded and admitted that this was a tough tale indeed.

"I've got to tell ya," the Texan shared with a note of concern. "I've really seen the game change out there for all my clients. It's shifted from all business is good business, to a real focus on profitability; we're in a totally new paradigm."

Jay's ears perked up and he chimed right in, "That paradigm thing is apparently what got me. She beat me out on profit contribution. Imagine that? We have always done whatever it took to keep business. You know; all that 'the customer is always right' stuff?"

Jay's newfound friend continued, "That mind-set is a lot like the Alamo, man; it is history, and most people think it went a lot better than it really did."

"To add insult to injury, it seems this person who is getting my award and my promotion has talked our president into locking us up with some negotiations *expert* for most of the next two days. Can you believe that? This clown is supposed to treat my 'negotiaphobia.' The guy is a doctor, so I guess he has come up with his own disease to treat. He has probably never sold one dime's worth of information management systems in his life, and he is going to tell us how to do it. Unbelievable! I end up in paradise, but I have to come home and explain to my friends and neighbors why I did not get one shade of tan."

With that, Jay took a quick glance at his watch and realized Laura would be tapping her toe as she waited for him in the hallway. She was always prompt, and he always got tied up in situations just like this one. Like his father, he never really encountered a stranger, only new friends. "Look, thanks for listening to me go on and on about my sudden disappointments. I am usually a better conversationalist than this. I am Jay Baxter. What is your name, my new friend from San Angelo?"

Both now standing, he told Jay, "My name is Pat, Patrick Perkins. Some of my students call me Dr. Pat; others have labeled me the One Minute Negotiator. They call me that because many of the ideas I give them only take a minute to do and really reduce their stress level after treating their 'negotiaphobia.' As I recall, you think I am a, what was it ... a clown? I'll see you first thing in the morning, Jay Baxter. By the way, Jay, you are never in the game too long to learn new skills. There are really no old dogs as long as they keep learning the new tricks."

CHAPTER 1 ONE MINUTE INSIGHTS

1. *Negotiaphobia* is a widespread and frequently unrecognized affliction that negatively impacts people in their personal and professional lives.
2. Today's business world is more challenging than ever before, but with good negotiation skills, positive results can be achieved.
3. Increasingly, business development professionals are being held accountable not only for revenue but for bottom-line profitability as well.

4. Until they chisel the second date on one's tombstone, it is never too late to learn, as we treat our negotiaphobia.

CHAPTER 2

Moonlight Reflections and Midcourse Corrections

That Darned Eduardo

Jay had hoped that just once Eduardo's grapevine would be wrong. Tonight, that was not the case. There stood Cathy Simmons with *his* golden statue. He had forewarned Laura of this possibility, and she was clearly crushed. He had to use all his powers of persuasion to even get her to go to the dinner. They ended up stuck at a table with no one they knew, and then the awful award ceremony. When President Blankenship made the announcement, over half the room looked immediately at Jay instead of Cathy.

One thing was definitely true about Jay: he was always the consummate professional. He smiled and appropriately applauded, even managing to drag himself to the front of the room after all the photos were taken and extend his hand to Cathy in congratulations. After the dinner, Bob Blankenship went out of his way to find Jay and personally compliment him on his year. "Jay, we are very pleased and proud to have you as a top performer on our team. You had a great year, and the events tonight don't change that. It was a very difficult decision for the executive committee, and be assured that you received a great deal of consideration and support." Jay thought, "Yeah, but not your support, and in the end that is the only factor that mattered."

Bob went on, "As you will hear when I kick off the negotiation workshop in the morning, we are shifting our strategy and focus to put a much greater emphasis on client profitability. I fully expect you to embrace the simple process you will be hearing about, and I would not be the least bit surprised to be handing that golden statue to you next year." Jay had always appreciated the way Bob could even put a happy face on an earthquake. And yes, his earth had been shaken in just a few short hours. This time, Bob's spin magic had not lasted longer than it took for him to glad-hand the next group of what Jay saw as "losers."

In Jay's world, there was no second place. He thought of the movie *Glengarry Glen Ross.* In that film about salespeople, first prize in a sales contest was a Cadillac, and second prize was a set of steak knives. He was left to wonder, "Where are my steak knives?" At that point, he realized he was better off not having ready access to any sharp objects.

The Rocking Boat

On top of everything else, Laura came down with a moderate case of sea sickness. Jay walked her back to the cabin and got her snugly into bed. He asked if she wanted him to stay with her, and she replied that she would be fine alone. "Go and enjoy your time with your friends, but don't be gone too long."

She was a trooper, but her disappointment was obvious and justified. Laura was classy and supportive enough to have avoided mentioning the impact of Cathy's victory on their new house plans. Jay knew that negotiation was on his horizon. He told himself that at least, unlike him, his wife had not expected the promotion. As he approached the door, she said, "I believe in you." He wondered what he could have ever done to deserve a woman like this as his soul mate.

Walking through the long narrow hallways of the ship, Jay was experiencing his own form of sickness—heartbreak. With both his son and daughter headed for college in the next few years, he knew he would soon also be suffering from "mal-tuition." After his unfortunate overly candid conversation with Dr. Pat earlier that evening, he was in no mood for company. He wished he could avoid even his own. Jay commiserated to himself, "To add insult to injury, I will have a target on my back over the next two days with that cowboy from Texas. Why did I open my big mouth to that guy? I am such an idiot!"

The Entire Bowl of Cherries

On the way out of the room, Jay had grabbed a pen and a legal pad. As he walked the deck, he looked for a relatively secluded lounge chair with enough light to allow him to make some notes.

Finding just the right spot in the glow of a brilliant full moon, he sat down to assess his lot in life. As Eduardo had reinforced, Jay thought of himself as a survivor. He had almost partied himself out of State University his freshman year. It took him five years to earn his undergrad degree, but he finished with a respectable GPA. When he accepted the position at XL, it was his third job after college. To start, Jay was given one of the weakest XL territories in the country. After he had built it up, five years ago he was rewarded with what was considered one of the company's "plum" territories.

Jay worked on both large and small accounts that, overall, generated an impressive record of annual revenue growth during his tenure, ranging from 9 to 19 percent, with an average growth rate in the midteens. The news of Cathy's impending promotion felt like a slap in the face. He asked himself, "What else could I have done?" At this point, he had no answers. "How had I missed the warning signs that this was going to happen?" he wondered.

As Jay started to reflect on his current lot in life, he first tried to focus on avoiding a pity party. He and Laura had been college sweethearts. They married the summer both graduated from State U. Times were never especially easy, but they always supported one another. In recent months, he had at times questioned that point as Laura was devoting more and more time to the community theater and had recently partnered with her sister to open a women's dress shop. With

Jay's travels of ten days a month or more, their relationship had evolved into one of voicemail, text messages, and sticky notes on the fridge. They used to schedule a "date night" at least once a month, but he was way behind on that pledge.

Jay was proud and thankful that he and Laura had two great kids. Their son, Trey, had just turned seventeen and was considered a solid, small-college baseball recruit, but probably not one who would be getting scholarship offers from any major universities. Their daughter, Ashley, was a story unto herself. She was now showing a strong interest in her social life, text messaging with abbreviations that would drive a court stenographer crazy, and buying designer handbags that created some major strain for the family credit cards. As he thought about the many negotiations in his life, he had to admit that his success rate was very low with his teenagers. To them "no" only meant "not yes yet" or a cue to simply change the parent they were negotiating with to an easier mark.

Jay was starting to realize the number and variety of negotiations he faced in his personal life. Just before the trip, his sister had expressed strong concern that their dad was starting to show some early signs of Alzheimer's disease. He was forgetting lots of small things, such as where he had parked his car at the airport the last time he returned from a trip to St. Martin. Jay felt that after Dad had spent several days relaxing in the Caribbean, they should expect him to forget what state he lived in, much less the whereabouts of his car. Jay tried to pass his sister's concerns off as a major overreaction, but she felt the symptoms were more serious and that they should be looking at medical specialists and assisted living options.

The Fork in the Road

Yogi Berra is renowned for saying, "When you come to a fork in the road, take it." Well, Jay felt like he was being stabbed by the fork in his road. He had several options at this point in his career, given the extreme disappointment experienced during his first evening of the so-called reward trip. He was now making some notes. First option: he could jump overboard. He was not serious, and this was not a survivor play.

Legitimate Option 1: he could look for a new job and perhaps even start in a management position. That idea seemed somewhat appealing. He had been approached by other companies in and outside the information systems management industry from time to time. There would be no Cathy Simmons in his life if he took this path. All the baggage that had been loaded on his career conveyor belt would immediately disappear. There were certainly positives to this option, but on the other side of the scale, he had invested so much of himself at XL that he hated to cut and run.

Option 2 centered on resisting this change in his company's strategy. He could muddle along as an average performer until the game changed back around. One part of him liked this path, but he had strong doubts as to whether it would actually work. Dr. Pat had mentioned that the focus on profitability was seemingly everywhere. Besides, *average* was not a word he ever wanted to associate with himself.

Option 3 was to chart a totally different course—not merely accepting, but fully embracing this change that had crashed into his life. He could take full advantage of this learning opportunity and make Bob Blankenship live his words about handing him the golden statue twelve months from now. Jay could make tonight's shocking events merely a bump in the road or, better yet, a wake-up call. "Tough times don't endure—tough people do," he told himself. If this Dr. Pat was right, he could make relatively minor changes in his process and generate big changes in his results.

If this were the new game for the business world, he could buy in and endeavor to learn from the person who was apparently the first in his company to treat her negotiaphobia. He could approach Dr. Pat first thing in the morning, let him know that he was there to learn and that he would be both an attentive and open-minded student. He could totally immerse himself in his treatment.

In less than a minute of scanning back over the three possible directions, Jay decided this final option was the most viable alternative and became committed not to just walking but sprinting down this path. He went so far as to write out and put his signature on this decision on a page in his legal pad. He was now totally committed.

CHAPTER 2 ONE MINUTE INSIGHTS

1. A gap in our negotiation skills can become apparent to us as a subtle tap on our shoulder; but to generate behavior change, it often requires a slap in the face.
2. Our past is the result of the experience we have gained and the decisions we have made, and our future will be shaped by our choices today and those yet to come.
3. Don't simply wait for the old game to return; learn the new one. The only constant is change, and the only real job security today is our own bank of relevant skill sets.
4. Life presents us with a series of learning opportunities. Should we decide to stop learning, we have begun our own obsolescence.

CHAPTER 3

The EASY Process for Treating Negotiaphobia

A New Day for Jay

As Jay climbed out of bed the next morning, he was fully committed to the one viable career option for him moving forward from this point in his life. He had read in a Ken Blanchard book that "people change when the pain not to change exceeds the pain to change." Jay had experienced his evening of pain, and his decision was to completely embrace the change that hit him yesterday like a slap in the face. He was committed to taking full advantage of the opportunity to learn what promised to be a simple process to treat his negotiaphobia and thus significantly enhance the profit contribution generated by his territory.

When Jay kissed an apparently fully recovered Laura good-bye, she told him to try to have a good day. He responded that he intended to have not just a good day but an outstanding day.

"What kind of transformation did you have last night?" Laura asked.

"I got a strong dose of perspective and reality. Love you, sweetheart," was Jay's smiling response as he waved good-bye, patted his heart as he always did for her, and then quietly closed the door.

The Doctor Is In

The banquet staff finishing the setup was the only sign of life in the meeting room when Jay arrived. When Dr. Patrick Perkins came through the door, this time in a shinier pair of cowboy boots, Jay approached him to modify the comments he had made the prior evening. As he walked up to the anointed "One Minute Negotiator," Dr. Pat cheerfully said, "Well, mornin', Mr. Jay Baxter. It looks like we are the early arrivals." Shaking hands, Jay began an explanation of his admitted learning reluctance from the prior evening.

Dr. Pat did not even allow him time to finish. "Don't concern yourself with the comments you shared last night. I probably should've let you know who I was, but I generally like to remain, shall we say, incognito, the evening before a session to get a read on people's attitudes as they approach the workshop. You'll see this morning that I start the meeting with a question to each of you concerning what you want out of this opportunity. Far and away the most honest answer I ever got was when one guy said, 'Me! Most of all I just want *me* out of this workshop.'" They both had a good laugh at that one. Dr. Pat told Jay to grab a good seat, and with that Jay put his materials on the table in the very front row.

The Charge to the Troops

Several minutes later when Eduardo entered the room, he scanned the scene and then walked over and asked Jay, "What are you doing way up here? There is no easy exit from this spot. You could catch something sitting this close." Jay smiled at his friend, saying, "It seems I've already caught negotiaphobia, and I'm here for my treatment. I saved this chair just for you, my friend." Frowning, Eduardo took the seat.

A few minutes later President Blankenship kicked off the workshop. His brief comments mirrored the ones he made to Jay the night before. They centered on the fact that the game had indeed changed. It was no longer strategically sound to evaluate each sales representative on top-line revenue and expect the company to magically generate the desired bottom-line profit. "We have always delivered exceptional value to our customers. The information systems that we work with them to design and implement are central to these organizations' overall success. It's definitely time to ensure that we are being fairly compensated for that value we are delivering. XL Information Solutions does not provide a commodity information management system, and we simply can't get paid as if we do. Our company's resources and your individual expertise are not unlimited, but are instead in finite supply. We need to be focusing on those customers who understand, appreciate, and are willing to pay for the exceptional work we do."

He went on, "Dr. Patrick Perkins is going to help us all recognize and develop a negotiation mind-set to do just that. I want to emphasize to all of you how much I am now using the unique process he shared with me in my negotiaphobia treatment about six months ago. The reason we have secured the services of Dr. Pat is that what he brings to us is easy to use, and much of it is useable in a minute or less. To give you an example, just last Wednesday I was involved in the final stages of a negotiation with one of our key suppliers. I was tempted to agree to what was a good counteroffer they had put on the table. Then I heard Dr. Pat's voice in my head saying, 'Give them a few seconds of silence and see what happens.' I did just that, and they kicked in an accommodation with regard to our payment terms that will free up capital and measurably impact XL's profitability. Give the One Minute Negotiator your absolute fullest attention, and understand there is *nothing,* and I mean nothing, more important you can possibly be doing over the next two days than being in here and learning what he has to share with you. Now, please join me in welcoming our seminar leader, Dr. Patrick Perkins." They all dutifully applauded, and Dr. Pat had the floor.

What Are We Talking About?

After some opening activities and the aforementioned identification of what each person wanted to gain from the two days, there was a brief discussion of the agenda for their time together. With that completed, Dr. Pat rapidly moved into the content of the workshop.

He pointed out that if the participants were going to effectively advance their negotiation process and skills, it would be essential to engage in a discussion of his description of the subject matter. His definition was already written on a flipchart:

> *A negotiation is the ongoing process through which two or more parties, whose positions are not necessarily consistent, work in an effort to reach an agreement.*

He called attention to the critical parts of this sentence. First was the word *process.* Dr. Pat stressed that most people think of a negotiation as an event that takes place only after the parties put their requests or positions on the table. In reality, negotiations are frequently an ongoing process, and those who focus strictly on the decision phase greatly reduce their effectiveness.

Dr. Pat clarified that the need identification and the postdecision implementation phases are often the most critical parts of the negotiation process. Then he asked what participants thought was the next significant component. Monte Beal from New York City brought up the multiple parties segment. Dr. Pat explained, "In a negotiation, there are both the people present and the people behind the scenes. Individuals behind the scenes are called constituents, and they often have more impact on what is said and done than the parties at the table."

The next components Dr. Pat discussed were the issues of inconsistent initial positions and working in an effort to reach an agreement. He said that as long as an agreement has not been reached, there is no guarantee there will ever be one. "I have watched what seemed to be very minor issues and small differences that were inappropriately handled kill a large deal. On the positive side, recognize that as long as the parties are talking to each other, there is still a chance for success. Even if they're yelling at you, at least they're still talking to you. The negotiation process is only dead when one or both sides permanently cease communications."

Dr. Pat further explained, "Differing initial positions are an often-misunderstood aspect of negotiations. If I am selling a car and you drive it and ask me how much I want for it, and I say $6,500, and you agree, that sounds like perfection, doesn't it?" He clarified that this means of reaching a deal is not actually a negotiation but rather an up-front agreement. While this sounds like perfection, ultimately it is likely that neither party would end up happy. "On the way home, you would probably begin to think that you paid too much and might have been able to buy the car for less. On the other side of the deal, when I go to the bank to deposit your check, I might start thinking that I could've gotten as much as $8,000 for the car; thus sensing that I left a lot of money on the table."

He paused for a moment to allow the participants to reflect on that logic, and then continued. "So you see, while an up-front agreement sounds like total bliss, it is in reality only through the time and effort we invest in a negotiation that we can reach an agreement both sides feel is in their best interests.

"By the way, almost all people overemphasize price in negotiations, just as in the car example I used. A savvy negotiator will tell you that if they let you set the price, and you let them set the terms, conditions, and deliverables, they will beat you every time. For example, the guy who agreed to buy the car might say, 'I'll pay that price, but only under the condition that it be repainted, with a new set of tires, a tune-up, and the payments spread out over two years.'" He explained that this could end up being a much better deal for the buyer than trying to get a somewhat lower cash price and then paying to have all of this work done.

The Epidemic of Negotiaphobia

Dr. Pat now shifted gears from what a negotiation is to why so many people fear the activity and even the term so much. "A majority of people today suffer from a stressful disease that is limiting their success and marginalizing the value they bring to their companies. It is so widespread that it has become an epidemic. 'Negotiaphobia' is the name I have given to this disease of attitude and skill deficiency. The symptoms involve not only the fear and loathing of negotiating, but also the willingness to live with the status quo instead of working to build more favorable outcomes. Signs of negotiaphobia include telling yourself that now is not the time to rock the boat. It is a longing for the 'good old days' when things were easier. I ask you to tell me of any day when people in business said, 'These are the good old days.' We have always faced challenges, and today isn't all that different."

Dr. Pat emphasized that the first issue in the treatment of this disease is to admit to yourself that you have these fears, feelings, and limitations. "By a show of hands, how many of you are willing to admit that you frequently fear and even sidestep negotiations that face you every day in every aspect of your life? Come on now, you will feel better after you admit it." Jay put not one but both his hands in the air, and with that, Eduardo broke out laughing.

Dr. Pat blamed two primary factors as negotiaphobia's disease agents. First, he indicated that many people see negotiations as acts of combat or conflict. "Most people just want to go along and get along. They hate uncertainty and rush to get any kind of agreement in place, even if it is a bad one. They do not want to butt heads and deal with what they feel are all the stress and hard feelings they think negotiations create.

"Let me share two different perspectives. First, it is not that difficult to overcome your negotiaphobia and become a proficient negotiator. Second, these negative feelings don't need to be prevalent and can often be controlled for many of the negotiations you engage in."

The second reason he provided for negotiaphobia reaching epidemic proportions was a general absence of investment in skill development. "How many of you have ever read a book or attended a workshop on negotiation skills—before today, that is?" Only Cathy Simmons and Bob Blankenship raised their hands. "This is the typical percentage I see day in and day out as I work with business professionals around the globe. Negotiating is an activity we find ourselves needing to engage in every day, but we seldom take the opportunity to invest time and funds to get better at it. Ladies and gentlemen, for all of you, the treatment for this disease begins right here and right now."

A Three-Step EASY Treatment Process

Dr. Pat next provided an overview of his simple process to treat the negotiaphobes. "Some people want to make the process of negotiating way too complex. Others try to oversimplify it and provide a one-size-fits-all approach. My 'clinic' follows the directive of a fairly smart fellow: Albert Einstein. He said, 'Make things as simple as possible, but no simpler.' The most exciting thing about this three-step process is that it simultaneously serves as a cure for negotiaphobia and the means to improving your negotiation results. This treatment process is easy yet powerful."

Dr. Pat now moved into the initial step. "The beginning of the three-step process for improving your negotiating is to *Engage* the treatment process. Let me be very clear that for each of you to start this process, you first must recognize that you are in a negotiation. A switch must flip in your head that tells you to engage the EASY process. With that switch flipped, you then progress through a quick mental review of the viable negotiation strategies. We will address *how* to negotiate by knowing and recognizing the different strategies shortly. Given my experience, I can spot when a situation calls for a negotiation and reflect through the various strategies very quickly. You'll be able to do the same by the time we conclude our discussions."

STEP 1

***Engage:* Recognize you are in a negotiation and quickly review the viable strategies.**

Dr. Pat next described the second phase of his prescribed treatment program. "In Step 2 of the treatment process, you *Assess* your negotiation strategy tendencies, as well as the tendencies of the other side or sides. Based on our basic nature and our experiences, we each come into any negotiation encounter with a higher or lower propensity to use each of the negotiation strategies. If we default to our comfort zone, get extremely lucky, and all the stars line up, it can work out okay for us. Unfortunately, for the untreated negotiaphobes, my experience has shown that all this comes together less than 20 percent of the time. That means that four out of five times people proceed with what is comfortable for them, but that provides a very low probability of success."

STEP 2

Assess: **Evaluate your tendency to use each of the negotiation strategies, as well as the tendencies of the other side(s).**

Dr. Pat continued, "In addition to knowing themselves, proficient negotiators quickly read the other side, because no one negotiates in a vacuum. There are at least two sides at the negotiation table, and you can only hope to control the side you are sitting on; and sometimes that is a big challenge. By becoming comfortable with this easy treatment process, much of the time you can quickly tell how they are likely to be negotiating with you.

"The third and final step is where you *Strategize* as you select the proper approach for this particular negotiation. In addition to considering yourself and the others at the table, this final step also takes into account the true significance of the opportunity. You simply pick the best approach, use it, monitor the impact, and then proceed or adjust based on the progress you are making. This learning experience is designed to result in your being proficient in all types of negotiations, so no matter what direction the other side goes in, you can strategize and effectively deal with it."

STEP 3

Strategize: **Slect the proper strategy for this particular negotiation.**

Bringing closure to the XL team's introduction of the three-step treatment, Dr. Pat asked, "How many of you find acronyms useful? Well, you may or may not have recognized it, but we just built a critical acronym that will take us through the rest of our time together. I promised you that treating negotiaphobia would be easy. Therefore, each time you are in a negotiation, if you will review the three steps as they pertain to the situation—which I call "Your One Minute Drill"—you will be more successful in your negotiations. By taking this minute for review you will definitely find this preparation to be a very handy tool, use better strategies and tactics, and become a proficient One Minute Negotiator.

"And to further help you overcome your negotia-phobia, here's an easy acronym to help you remember the process: E-A-S-Y: Engage, Assess, Strategize, and Your One Minute Drill. If Dr. Pat promises you easy, he is darn sure going to give you E-A-S-Y."

Your One Minute Drill: **Each time you begin a negotiation situation, take a minute to review the three steps.**

Dr. Pat continued to give the XL participants even more confidence about the journey they had just begun. "In a very short period of time, the One Minute Drill will become second nature to you; you will do it naturally. How many of you had to think about putting on your seat belt the first time you drove a car?" All the hands went up. "Okay, how many of you have to think about it now?" There were only smiles around the room. "The One Minute Drill is your negotiation seat belt."

Stepping Up

"The one question about the three-step process I hear most often is, which one of the steps is most important? My smart-aleck answer is 'The one you skip. The one that trips you when you run back upstairs at your house to get your keys is the one you failed to take into account.' It is the same with negotiations. The truth is, the first step, to engage, has to be the most important. If the switch in your head does not flip and you have no clear understanding of the viable strategies for negotiating, the easy negotiaphobia treatment process never even begins. This certainly does not mean you can shortchange the other two steps as you do your drill."

As Dr. Pat approached the conclusion of the first session, he got very serious in making a promise to the group. "I'll guarantee that if all of you will focus on learning how to do these three easy steps well, you will become proficient negotiators. Let me quickly clarify what makes for a proficient negotiator. You will effectively control your negotiaphobia and enjoy a high level of success in reducing your stress and generating the outcomes you are seeking in your negotiations. You will also become more efficient, consuming no more resources, including your time, than is required in producing these superior results. With only limited consideration and practice, you will be able to cycle through these steps and do them in only one minute. When you reflect on successful negotiations, you will give credit to the use of this process. When things do not turn out so well, you should immediately reexamine the process used to see which steps might have been overlooked or not appropriately executed. Now, go get some pastries and coffee and be back in fourteen and a half minutes."

CHAPTER 3 ONE MINUTE INSIGHTS

1. A negotiation occurs when two or more parties have perceived differences in positions and put forth the effort to close gaps and reach an agreement.
2. As with most diseases, the first issue in treating negotiaphobia is to admit you have it.
3. People fear negotiating for two primary reasons: a widespread lack of skill, and a misunderstanding of the nature of the process leading to a misguided desire to avoid conflict.
4. The treatment of negotiaphobia is an easy process that begins with Engaging, as you review what a negotiation is and your strategy options; Assessing your own tendencies and the tendencies of the other side; and then Strategizing to identify what approach is the best fit for the situation. The review of these steps comprises Your One Minute Drill that should drive your process for every negotiation.

CHAPTER 4

Engaging the Treatment Process

Attitude Is Everything

Back in their seats, Eduardo and Jay had a moment for a short chat. Eduardo was clearly feeling more positive about things. "Jay, it is still too early to tell for certain, but it seems this guy is going to be okay. I am hoping that his easy process is as simple and quick as he says it is. I started out reading a negotiation book one time, and everything seemed so complex. Who can remember twenty-five or thirty things when you are under the gun?" Jay agreed with his friend, adding that if there was a way to reduce the mounting level of stress in all areas of his life, he was all ears. Eduardo teased, "Jay, that is scary, because you have some monster ears."

After the break, Dr. Pat returned to Step 1 of the EASY *negotiaphobia* treatment process. Knowing what a negotiation is and recognizing that they were in one, the XL team would now consider the four viable negotiation strategies.

"One thing I have come to recognize in working with negotiators," Dr. Pat began, "is that they frequently make the mistake of jumping to a tactic without having even thought about what strategy would work best. They kick out a price point or make a demand that often turns the entire process in the wrong direction. They may really want to go to LA, but they just boarded a flight to JFK. Just remember that your strategy is the direction you choose, and your tactics are the moves you will make to get there."

On the screen, Dr. Pat provided a visual for the group reminding them that they were still in Step 1 of the treatment process, as the top three boxes were now shaded in gray.

Your One Minute Drill: Each time you begin a negotiation situation, take a minute to review the three steps.

STEP 3

Strategize: Select the proper strategy for this particular negotiation.

38

> # STEP 2
>
> *Assess:* Evaluate your tendency to use each of the negotiation strategies, as well as the tendencies of the other side(s).

> # STEP 1
>
> ***Engage:*** **Engage: Recognize you are in a negotiation and quickly review the viable strategies.**

© U.S. Learning

Confusion about Compromise

Before beginning his discussion of the four strategies, Dr. Pat told the group there was one common technique that people frequently use to negotiate and that everyone needed to gain a fresh and more appropriate perspective on. He claimed that compromise causes more confusion about the nature of negotiations than any other issue. He proposed that this is the most used and abused tactic in negotiations. "In most instances, compromise shouldn't really come under the heading of how to negotiate, but rather how *not* to negotiate. Let me emphasize that compromise is *not* a legitimate strategy to use in considering and approaching a negotiation. It is one of those premature tactical plays I mentioned, and I am here and now cautioning you about its use."

Dr. Pat defined compromise as a mathematical calculation used to split the difference between the differing positions taken by the sides in a negotiation. He revisited the car sale example, stating that if he were asking $7,000 and the buyer offered $5,000, then compromise would have us add the two numbers together and divide by two. This makes the number $6,000.

"The excuse people give for using compromise is a desire to make everyone happy. Well, if the buyer really believed the car was only worth $5,000 and paid $1,000 more than that, she would not be very happy. Likewise, the seller would not be content with $1,000 below what he felt was a justified price."

Dr. Pat added some clarification before leaving the topic of compromise as a factor in Step 1 of engaging the process. "I don't want you to leave this topic thinking that compromise is always a bad tactic. It does have its place, and here is what I would like for you to remember to help you use it properly. Compromise should only be used late in the negotiation process, after legitimate negotiation strategies have been selected and fully used, when only a small gap in positions remains for just one issue, and it should always be directly tied to an agreement. If you use it under these circumstances, it can be a valuable tactic for reaching an agreement." Many of the participants quickly recognized that they had prematurely jumped to this tactic in many of their negotiations.

The 2 × 2 Negotiation Matrix

Dr. Pat's tone now became much more serious than at any point so far. "I want you to be highly aware that engaging your treatment for negotiaphobia must be grounded in an understanding of the four legitimate negotiation strategies. After working in this skill area for about a decade, on a coast-to-coast flight one night, I pulled out a tablet and pen to see if I could better lay out and demonstrate the relationship between the various ways negotiations unfold. After four bags of pretzels, considerable frustration, and a number of wasted pages, I came to the conclusion that negotiation strategies can best be evaluated and more easily understood by looking at two important dimensions: activation and cooperation."

He then asked the participants, "As a child, when one of your parents came into a room where you and a sibling were fighting, what was the first question they asked?"

Several of them immediately verbalized their response: "Who started it?!"

"That," he said, "is the essence of understanding activation." On a flip chart, he drew a vertical line with the labels *reactive* at the bottom and *proactive* at its top. He went on to explain that proactive parties in a negotiation are willing to initiate and advance the process, while reactive parties only respond to what the other side has said or done. Dr. Pat proposed that in a large percentage of situations, it is far better to be proactive when a negotiation is needed to address differences. He indicated that sitting back and waiting for things to take care of themselves seldom works out well, referencing his earlier comments about negotiaphobia and people continuing to live with an inadequate and often deteriorating status quo. Jay found himself reflecting on his relationship with his sister and their exchange surrounding the health of their father. She had been the proactive one, while Jay now realized he had not even been appropriately reactive.

Dr. Pat next turned his attention to the second dimension of the matrix: cooperation. He stated, "In considering negotiation strategies, to varying degrees, people are either low or high on this dimension." This time he drew a horizontal line on the flip chart that cut the activation line in half. "*Low Cooperation* negotiators (on the left side) are only out for themselves and focused on their own agenda, while *High Cooperation* negotiators (on the right side) demonstrate an interest in understanding and attempting to address not only their own issues and needs, but those of the other side or sides as well."

42

The Negotiation Strategy Matrix

Proactive

Competition	**Collaboration**
Avoidance	**Accommodation**

Low
Cooperation

High
Cooperation

Reactive

© U.S. Learning

As the participants were finishing their own drawing, he said, "You probably want to know what words go in the four boxes we just created by intersecting the two lines. Well, we now have a simple means to position the four legitimate negotiation strategies in a way that should clarify the nature of the strategy or strategies that can be used in any negotiation situation."

Heads in the Sand

"The first strategy we will consider is *Avoidance.* I would like to put it off for later, but I can't." After a short pause for effect, Dr. Pat got a nice laugh out of the one-liner. "This is a reactive and low-cooperation approach (lower left), and this box in the matrix was given the color gray on the projected graphic because it is a negotiation strategy that's in the gray area of not overtly negotiating at all. This is the strategy uncontrolled negotiaphobes will default to a high percentage of the time.

"An animal for you to visualize when it comes to avoidance is an ostrich," Dr. Pat said. "The darn thing puts its head in the sand when facing a threat. No wonder it is one of the few birds that can't fly. Usually, this strategy does not fly well either. People often use the alibi that they don't have the time right now to deal with this issue. Let me share a secret with you: you don't have the time *not* to deal with and resolve important issues. There are instances where avoidance is a fit, but we will discuss those circumstances a bit later."

Wanting to even the score, Jay passed Eduardo a short note: "Is that sand I see behind your right ear, big guy?"

Controlling the Bleeding

Next, Dr. Pat pointed toward *Accommodation* in the lower-right box on his matrix, indicating that this is a reactive strategy accompanied by a high level of cooperation. He explained that it was assigned the color yellow because, like the midpoint on a stoplight, accommodation is a strategy that should only be used with great caution. Dr. Pat described accommodation as basically giving in and providing, or allowing the other side to take, what they are asking for.

"After you run out of gas in the middle of west Texas and a tow truck with a full ten-gallon gas can drives up, you'll most definitely be accommodating on price and pretty much anything else, and properly so," he said. "It happened to me once, and the driver didn't accept credit cards. I was out of cash. I think he is still wearin' my first Rolex." The group roared with laughter.

"When you're accommodating, you are bleeding from the wrist." He asked if there were any former Boy Scouts or Girl Scouts in the group. Jay raised his hand, and before he realized it blurted out, "I was an Eagle Scout." Dr. Pat asked him what he would place above his elbow, if he were cut and bleeding from the wrist. Reflecting back several decades, Jay answered, "A tourniquet to control the blood flow." Years ago he had actually used a large handkerchief for a tourniquet as he tied it around a friend's arm near the elbow when the fellow scout had accidentally sliced his forearm on sharp rock. Dr. Pat clarified for the group that in negotiations, understanding that we are in fact accommodating is our "tourniquet" that will restrict the flow of money or other resources we have to give to the other side to get or retain a deal.

"Armed with this knowledge, we must recognize the need to only accommodate with great care to ensure we don't find ourselves in the same position with the same party in the future. In order to work toward a more favorable situation, you need to either strengthen your position with this party, or find another option before negotiating with 'em again," he advised.

"A very common mistake people make in negotiations is to think they can *build* relationships via accommodation," Dr. Pat explained. "That's like putting a saucer of cream outside your back door to drive a stray cat away. Tomorrow, that critter will be back, with lots of friends." He indicated that as a strategy, accommodation only allows you to *test* relationships. If the other side takes advantage of you when you're accommodating, you learn that you didn't have a relationship in the first place.

At this point, Jay realized that he had accommodated quite frequently with several of his customers, and most of the time he had not even recognized what he was actually doing or the long-term consequences. He had convinced himself that it would save him time to simply agree and move on. Just two weeks ago, he had agreed to provide a system upgrade for free to a large Cleveland law firm. He now recognized that this "saucer of cream" would be shared with their friends at other firms that used XL, and it would be more difficult to charge for similar upgrades in the future. This was another epiphany for Jay!

The Zero-Sum Game

Next, Dr. Pat shifted the group's attention upward to the top half of the four-quadrant grid and its two proactive strategies. "One sign you are managing your negotiaphobia is a shift in focus from the bottom half of the matrix to the top half. This is due to the general ability of the top two strategies to more frequently reduce your stress and generate superior results."

Pointing to the top-left quadrant, he began the discussion of *Competition.* He said that the color in this box should be associated with a flashing red light, where we should stop, think, and only proceed with a careful consideration of the situation at hand.

He continued, "Competition is a win-lose strategy driven by knowledge, skills, and nerve. When you employ this strategy, you're engaged in a zero-sum game. This means the only way you can get a dollar is to take one away from the other side, and likewise, that party is trying to take that very same money away from you. The size of the pie is fixed, so you're only really fighting over the size of your slice."

He stated that when someone is using a competitive strategy, they are in essence saying there is no real relationship. He again used the example of the tow truck driver in the desert who knows he has not seen the stranded driver before and likely will never see him again. "So his mind-set is to get the most out of this gas-for-cash transaction that he possibly can," Dr. Pat explained. "You don't worry about damaging the relationship. You can't damage something that does not exist. It would be like me worrying about wrecking my Austin Healey Roadster. That is simply not possible. I might want one, but I ain't got one. Have you priced those suckers lately?" Eduardo now knew another reason why Bob Blankenship liked Dr. Pat so much. That very car was the XL president's prized possession. He was not willing to believe this analogy was an accident. This gringo from west Texas had definitely done his homework.

Playing Win-Win

Everyone in the room now knew where Dr. Pat would head next: the top-right quadrant, signifying proactivity combined with a high level of cooperation. He emphasized that this last alternative is the most advanced of the four strategies. "This is because in such instances, the negotiation is based on all parties' true *needs,* not simply the positions being stated. It's a win-win strategy because now the focus lies in the possibility of growing the size of the pie, not just trying to grab a larger slice. The key to getting the needs and capabilities on the table to make this happen is the creation of a problem-solving environment where everyone feels comfortable openly sharing this information, and then jointly developing solutions that have the potential to meet those needs."

Dr. Pat asked if anyone in the room would take 1 percent of a deal. Most people immediately shook their head. Then he asked, "How about 1 percent of a trillion-dollar deal? Would you take $10 billion?" Now all the participants were smiling and nodding. Jay thought that with even the smallest fraction of that total, he could pay cash for a new house that would exceed even Laura's expectations.

Dr. Pat continued his discussion of the virtues of collaboration. "Problem solving to create a super option capable of delivering an exceptional outcome has to be the expectation behind collaboration. If this were not a possibility, this strategy would simply not be worth the exposure and investment of time and effort."

He indicated that from his experience, true collaboration, while generally desirable, is pretty rare. "Based on the people I've encountered and the deals I have worked on, only about 20 percent of humans can effectively collaborate. While really not all that complex, it is not a natural skill, but rather a capability that must be learned and developed. Since the time of cavemen, we have been wired to take care of ourselves, and that is not necessarily a bad thing. Proficient negotiators have developed an advanced capability to maximize the benefit of all parties involved. By tomorrow afternoon, you can grab your place in that group of most advanced negotiators, if you wish to do so."

Exercise Time

With the matrix filled in, Dr. Pat gave the group a twenty-minute break that included an exercise essential in starting Step 2 of their treatment of negotiaphobia. Eduardo and most of the other participants were gone in a flash, but Jay spent at least five of those minutes making additional notes about the nature of the four strategies. On his way out of the room, he asked Dr. Pat why people so easily slide into avoidance.

"Jay, negotiaphobes seem to simply buy into that old adage that time heals all ills. From my experience, time doesn't heal much of anything that is negatively impacting a relationship. Such problems, personal and business alike, are like bumps on a steer. You just have to step up, acknowledge their existence, and lance the darn things. The process is not all that appealing, but everything is so much better when you're done."

Jay walked off with one nagging question: "Where does this guy come up with this stuff?" He vowed to learn and utilize the easy process and no longer settle for a marginal status quo in a high-potential business relationship. He began to think about one particular client in Camden, Ohio, that was at the very top of his collaborative opportunities list. It was not a bad customer, but he was sensing it could be so much better for both sides with a collaborative strategy in place. He would also place a call to his sister as soon as they docked in Miami. There was no other option than to collaborate with her over their dad's growing loss of memory. He was no longer in avoidance-based denial.

CHAPTER 4 ONE MINUTE INSIGHTS

1. Compromise is not a legitimate negotiation strategy. It is a frequently used, often abused tactic that is important to recognize, understand, and use selectively.
2. The four legitimate negotiation strategies of avoidance, accommodation, competition, and collaboration can each be better understood when considering their respective levels of activation and cooperation.
3. Competition is about fighting to get a larger slice of the pie, while collaboration focuses on growing the size of the pie.
4. In most negotiation encounters, the two proactive strategies of competition and collaboration tend to generate superior results when compared with either of the reactive strategies of avoidance and accommodation.

CHAPTER 5

Assessing Your Tendencies

A Disturbing Revelation

As they were returning to their seats, many of the XL participants were commenting that they had never really thought about looking at negotiations from the perspective of the four strategies. They also were recognizing the prevalence of negotiations in their business or personal lives. Even Eduardo had to admit that despite a successful sales career, he had been a practicing negotiaphobe.

Before giving the participants their break, Dr. Pat had asked each of them to start Step 2 of their negotiaphobia treatment process (assess) by completing his twenty-question negotiation self-assessment questionnaire. This would begin their journey toward more completely understanding themselves and their tendencies when it comes to how they negotiate. By the time they returned, they were to have marked their first reaction (one to seven levels of agreement) to each of the twenty comments.

Your One Minute Drill: Each time you begin a negotiation situation, take a minute to review the three steps.

STEP 3

Strategize: Select the proper strategy for this particular negotiation.

STEP 2

Assess: Evaluate your tendency to use each of the negotiation strategies, as well as the tendencies of the other side(s).

STEP 1

Engage: Recognize you are in a negotiation and quickly review the viable strategies.

The self-assessment Dr. Pat gave the XL participants is presented here, and the authors strongly recommend that you complete it at this time. Please do not avoid this activity, as you will diminish your learning process. If you do not want to write in your book, copy the assessment, and do it on separate sheets.

OMN Negotiation Strategy Self-Assessment Scale

Assess your negotiation strategy tendencies. Read each statement carefully; then circle the extent to which the statement describes your approach when it comes to negotiating with key internal and external parties.

Answer Key

1. Completely uncharacteristic
2. Uncharacteristic
3. Somewhat uncharacteristic
4. Neither characteristic nor uncharacteristic
5. Somewhat characteristic
6. Characteristic
7. Completely characteristic

Circle the number that you initially feel most applies to you for each statement below:

1. When I negotiate, my interests must prevail.
   1 2 3 4 5 6 7
2. I often find reasons to put off meetings until a better time, even when there is a chance discussions might help resolve a dispute.
   1 2 3 4 5 6 7

3. It is smart to put aside unpleasant confrontations and negotiate using a friendly approach.
   1 2 3 4 5 6 7

4. The focus of the negotiation should be to get as large a "slice of the pie" as possible.
   1 2 3 4 5 6 7

5. I try to identify shared principles to use as a basis for resolving disputes.
   1 2 3 4 5 6 7

6. Often the best approach is to just do what you need to do and hope the other side does not notice.
   1 2 3 4 5 6 7

7. I will often give up things to the other party in an effort to advance our relationship.
   1 2 3 4 5 6 7

8. I often live with marginal solutions to avoid having to negotiate a new deal with this or another party.
   1 2 3 4 5 6 7

9. My approach is to try to get more than half of the money on the table.
   1 2 3 4 5 6 7

10. The best way to buy things today is to get a product and price off the Internet so I don't have to negotiate with a real person.
    1 2 3 4 5 6 7

11. I try to get the deal done by finding a way to give the other party what they are asking for.
    1 2 3 4 5 6 7

12. "Take more than you give" is my motto.
   1 2 3 4 5 6 7
13. Effective negotiators often seek to develop a true partnership with the other parties involved.
   1 2 3 4 5 6 7
14. I frequently feel that I fail to get what I want from a negotiation because the other side is "holding most of the cards."
   1 2 3 4 5 6 7
15. By using discovery to get past positions and down to true needs, one can reduce or eliminate unproductive and time-consuming conflicts.
   1 2 3 4 5 6 7
16. You should do unto others before they do it to you.
   1 2 3 4 5 6 7
17. When negotiating, I attempt to work through our differences and build on common ground.
   1 2 3 4 5 6 7
18. I attempt to develop an opening proposal so attractive that the other party will simply accept it.
   1 2 3 4 5 6 7
19. The best thing about doing business based on long-term personal relationships is that it significantly reduces my need to discuss prices and deliverables.
   1 2 3 4 5 6 7

56

Question Number	Avoidance	Accommodation	Competition	Collaboration
1				
2				
3				
4				
5				
6				
7				
8				
9				
10				
11				
12				
13				
14				
15				
16				
17				
18				
19				
20				
TOTAL				

©2010 U.S. Learning

20. You get better negotiation outcomes when you keep people's emotions in check and work to uncover everyone's true needs.

1 2 3 4 5 6 7

Scoring Your Answers: Once you have circled the most appropriate number for all twenty questions, please transfer your score for each question into the only white box next to the corresponding question number. Once this is done, total all four vertical columns, and record your scores in the proper blank at the bottom of this page.

Note your total score for each:

Avoidance: _____ Accommodation: _____

Collaboration: _____ Competition: _____

What Does It All Mean?

Dr. Pat restarted the workshop by saying, "Now that we have defined and briefly considered the four legitimate negotiation strategies, most of you are likely asking an important question. That question is 'Am I an avoider, accommodator, competitor, or collaborator?' The answer to this question is ... *yes.* We all have some leanings toward all four strategies ingrained in us. It is simply a matter of degree, so it is essential that we assess which strategy is likely to be dominant for each of us."

Dr. Pat stressed that the reality of the tool being a *self-assessment* naturally had some impact on the validity of the results. He encouraged each participant to share the scale with people who know them best, including friends, family members, coworkers, and customers.

Me? Avoid? I Don't Even Want to Talk about It

The One Minute Negotiator started the interpretation of the results with the first column, avoidance.

"By a show of hands, how many of you had your highest of the four assessment scores in avoidance?" No one raised their hand. "Well, the record is still intact." The group was told that everyone naturally underreports the extent to which they are an avoider as part of not wanting to admit to this level of the affliction of negotiaphobia. "True avoiders would not even complete the scale in the first place. I use a different scoring system to judge anyone's avoidance tendency. A number as high as in the low teens should cause that person to recognize he or she is likely overusing this strategy."

Jay looked down at his total for avoidance. It was 15, which just served to strengthen his ongoing recognition of his propensity to be an avoider, an ostrich.

The "Grading" Scale

For the next three columns, Dr. Pat shared with the participants the following scale to help them interpret their self-assessment results from the grid page. "Having been a college professor in an earlier life, I see no reason not to stay with a 90, 80, 70, 60 percentage approach to evaluating these results."

32 – 35	An extremely strong tendency to use this strategy
28 – 31	A strong tendency to use this strategy

25 – 27	A moderate tendency to use this strategy
21 – 24	A low tendency to use this strategy
32 – 35	An extremely strong tendency to use this strategy
18–20	An extremely low tendency to use this strategy
17 and below	strong tendency not to use this strategy (with the exception of avoidance

Is It Really Better to Give Than to Receive?

Now moving on to the second column, Dr. Pat inquired how many people had their highest score for accommodation. About 15 percent of the participants raised their hands, looking somewhat sheepish as they did so.

"This is the proportion of participants I normally see for accommodation, and at this initial step in understanding your negotiaphobia, let me emphasize that there is nothing wrong with having your strongest tendency associated with this strategy. As I said earlier, many people assume that accommodation is the natural way to build relationships." He indicated that once the participants understand the role for all four negotiation strategies, they will realize that this is *not* the case. They will step back and determine the proper path to generate the best possible outcomes in the least amount of time.

Jay was feeling good that his number for accommodation was only 25—a moderate tendency, but not the highest of his four scores. Jay's other neighbor, Andrew, had been one of the people to raise his hand. "This guy has more cats outside his back door than anyone else for miles around," Jay thought.

Battlers—Few and Far Between

Moving to the third column from the left, Dr. Pat asked who among the group had their highest assessment score on competition. Two people put their hands up. It was hard not to notice that they were two of the youngest participants in the group and that both of them were men. When Dr. Pat asked about their backgrounds, both indicated they were recent MBA graduates and were early in their first jobs in the business world. One admitted to scoring a 29 on the competitive scale, and the other a 28. Dr. Pat then commented that these two participants are prototypical of participants scoring highest on the competitive scale. He said they tend to be younger, are more likely to be male, and are often fresh out of graduate business school, where a survival-of-the-fittest mindset tends to prevail.

As Jay looked at his 20 score on competition, he wished it could have been at least one point higher. That single point would have moved him into the low-tendency category. "I can't be this much of a wimp," he told himself. Andrew bragged that he beat Jay with a 22. Jay immediately moved to hide his scores a bit more carefully. He wondered if maybe he could go back and change one answer by a point or two.

It was at that very moment, Dr. Pat warned the group, "I see many of you looking back over the twenty statements and your own level of agreement for them. It is logical to want to rework some of your responses, but this is not the point. Everyone conducts their own evaluations a little differently. The key issue for you will be to compare these results with the ones you generate when you retake the self-assessment in a couple of months."

The Wannabe Winners

He then moved to the final category. "Many of you need some exercise, so at this point, everyone having their highest score on collaboration, put your hands up." Everyone but the accommodators and competitors raised their hands. Dr. Pat explained that this result is very representative of prior groups for a number of reasons. First, the five collaborative statements just sound like comments you *should* agree with. "The collaborative items tend to come across to many participants like I love my mom, apple pie, and the flag. This is a self-assessment evaluation, and it is difficult not to answer the way we *wish* we thought and behaved. That is why I encourage you to have others who know you do an assessment based on their perceptions of you." He stated that what really matters as we negotiate is how the other side sees us. That impression has the largest influence on how they negotiate with us. "So, I suppose this second treatment step is really to 'know yourself as others know you.'"

Dr. Pat went on to say that the best negotiators he has worked with score highest on collaboration, and he does so himself as well. He made the point that his biggest concern was when the number for any strategy was too high. Jay, and apparently most of the rest of the participants, found this to be a puzzling comment. He thought, "How can someone be too collaborative?" He had been smiling broadly about his score of 32, but now his expression had changed. Carly from Seattle asked why a very high collaboration number should be a concern. "Did you not say that this strategy often generates the best possible negotiation outcomes?" she asked.

Dr. Pat nodded in agreement and then expounded. "The real challenge with an extremely strong tendency is that as the number gets up into the 30s, you may deploy this strategy irrespective of the situation or the strategy being used by the other side. This is the main difference between two categories of collaborators I now see as existing. The first group is what I call sages. A sage takes a minute to recognize when to collaborate and when this is not the best strategy. The second set of collaborators is made up of dreamers. These people try to be collaborative in each negotiation encounter, hoping the other side or sides will reciprocate." He went on to ask the group, if they were collaborating and the other side was competing, what would they *actually* be doing?

One person on the left side of the room loudly said, "Accommodating." It was another epiphany for many in the group.

"That is right. And what don't you have at your elbow due to the use of the unintentional use of this strategy?"

Jay mumbled to himself, "A tourniquet."

Dr. Pat clarified that the aspects of a problem-solving environment both sides find essential when they are collaborating, such as asking questions about needs and demonstrating flexibility and creativity, are actually seen as weaknesses to be exploited by the other side when they are competing with a collaborator. "When the other side determines that they will use a competitive strategy, unless you can move to change their mind, you simply no longer have the option of collaborating. You can avoid, accommodate, or compete with them, and maybe appropriately try the late-game compromise tactic, but you simply can no longer collaborate. Unilateral collaboration is de facto accommodation." Everyone took one minute to write that warning down. It was a major take-away.

Now Jay wasn't at all certain whether he was a pure accommodator or simply a dreamer. At this point, he didn't necessarily believe there was that much of a difference between the two in terms of their negative consequences. He may well have accommodated too much with several of his clients in recent years; most notably a customer called MGB Properties. He leaned back and stared at the ceiling wondering how much of his and XL's money he had left on the table.

The Critical Comparison

Having addressed the assessment score interpretations for all four negotiation strategies in the matrix, Dr. Pat now moved to what he said was the most important assessment in order to glean some useful intelligence from the four data points.

"As far as I am concerned, the most important Step 2 revelation to be gained from the totals you generated in completing your self-assessment is the relationship between Columns 2 and 3. How many of you had your competition score higher than your accommodation score?" About one-fifth of the participants raised their hands; neither Jay nor Eduardo were in the group, but Cathy and Bob were.

Dr. Pat continued this discussion with a new level of seriousness in his voice to take all participants' self-awareness to the next level. "This outcome has been shown to be a major characteristic of a proficient negotiator. When the other side goes competitive, and you are actually more likely to compete than to simply give in, and the other side promptly and clearly *recognizes* this tendency, you will be given many more collaborative opportunities." He stated that this is because most of the time when the other side goes competitive, they do *not* expect to face competition in return. If they expect or experience reciprocal competition, they may intelligently adjust their strategy and work with the other side in a more collaborative fashion.

Dr. Pat continued, "When my business partner and I first started helping people develop their negotiation skills well over a decade ago, we did not include competitive skills and tactics in our curriculum. That was because we both firmly believed, and had experienced, that a collaborative approach generates more favorable overall outcomes than a win-lose fixed-pie competitive approach. Then we started to realize that without the presence of a strong competitive skills base, the other side will see you as 'low-hanging fruit' and go competitive against you almost every time." Jay was feeling that his MGB Properties customer saw him as easy pickings for its aggressive and highly competitive purchasing practices.

Dr. Pat went on to give the participants what he felt would be the best news they would get all day. "Keep in mind that you do not need to complete this twenty-statement assessment in Step 2 every time you go through the EASY treatment process. I do recommend that at least once a quarter for the next year or so, you retake it. Early on in your treatment, some assessment numbers tend to shift over time.

"Irrespective of your present set of assessment scores on the accommodation and competition strategies, experience with thousands of participants similar to you has shown that as a person uses the three-step process to treat his or her negotiaphobia, two very positive results emerge rather quickly." The first favorable outcome Dr. Pat identified was that people's accommodation tendency normally goes down fairly dramatically after recognizing that by giving the other side what they are asking for, they are not building a true relationship. Instead, they recognize they are showing weaknesses to someone focused on preying on weak opponents.

"A second positive is that as participants understand competition and get more comfortable with it, their tendency to use a win-lose approach goes up. They recognize the opportunity for quick victories with this strategy." Dr. Pat cautioned that the biggest challenge he has faced after some participants completed this workshop was the pendulum swinging so far to the top left of the matrix that a number of people actually become *overly* competitive.

Advancing by Adapting

The One Minute Negotiator continued his explanation of Step 2 of the three-step treatment of negotiaphobia. "We have invested a good deal of time in this session to help you assess yourself and your negotiation strategy tendencies. Now that you have invested this time in understanding your tendencies, it will only take a moment to think about what your comfort zone is and see that as a match or a miss for the negotiation at hand. Negotiaphobes not only avoid negotiations; they also demonstrate disease symptoms by their unwillingness to move outside their comfort zone in terms of how they negotiate. You must increase your adaptability if you are to increase your rate of success."

Setting up the next segment, he stated, "One issue that will cause you to adapt is your anticipation of, and response to, the strategy being used by the other side. This is a major factor in strategizing which of the four strategies to deploy. We will move into that issue as we continue with the second step of your treatment for negotiaphobia."

As they got up to leave the room, Jay and Eduardo looked at each other and simply said, "Wow." It was hard for them to believe how much the self-assessment had taught them about themselves and how they had naturally and frequently inappropriately negotiated. Make no mistake: sitting on a beach today would have been more enjoyable. With what they were learning, however, they just might be able to go in together and buy that beach house they rented last spring in Key Largo.

CHAPTER 5 ONE MINUTE INSIGHTS

1. Most negotiaphobes use the avoidance negotiation strategy much more frequently than they realize or care to admit.
2. The most successful negotiators generally have a strong collaborative tendency, but not so

strong that they always blindly deploy this strategy as a dreamer.

3. The stronger our comfort with and skill in using a competitive approach, the more collaborative opportunities will develop for us.

4. As we treat our negotiaphobia, our accommodation tendency usually declines and our propensity to compete increases.

CHAPTER 6

Assessing the Tendencies of Others

Dealing with the Other Side

Dr. Pat was now ready for the phase of taking the XL participants into the outward-focused portion of Step 2 in their treatment for negotiaphobia: assessing the other side's strategic tendencies. Both Jay and Eduardo found it odd that their leader started the afternoon session of the workshop holding a deck of cards. Eduardo jokingly asked, "Hey, Doc, we going to play Texas Hold 'Em or what?" Dr. Pat simply shuffled the deck and smiled.

Your One Minute Drill: Each time you begin a negotiation situation, take a minute to review the three steps.

Strategize: Select the proper strategy for this particular negotiation.

STEP 2

Assess: Evaluate your tendency to use each of the negotiation strategies, as well as the tendencies of the other side(s).

STEP 1

Engage Recognize you are in a negotiation and quickly review the viable strategies.

You Ain't Playin' Solitaire

"Well, now that you are well versed on the four strategies, and which ones *you* are most likely to use, you have a pretty good view of how you like to play your negotiation cards. Like Eduardo just mentioned, a lot of people rightly think of negotiations as a high-stakes card game. But as we all know, unless you are playing solitaire, there are other people at the card table, and they are not simply filling a seat to watch you win. They want the game to go well for them, and they have their own negotiation strategy tendencies. Your ability to effectively assess them and anticipate how they like to play, when coupled with knowing how you like to play, will take you a long way down the road toward generating successful negotiation outcomes."

The need to know how everyone at the negotiation table likes to play cards sounded like a daunting task to Jay. He was already concerned about becoming tougher and less of an accommodator. Now he had to get inside the heads of the other people involved?

That is when Dr. Pat stepped in to address Jay's rapidly developing fears. "I am seeing frowns on some of your faces. This all sounds tough, doesn't it? I told you I was going to make this easy for you. Allow me to let you in on a little secret. Most people are extremely predictable when it comes to how they negotiate, and even those who aren't rarely have a good enough poker face to effectively hide the strategy they are using for very long. After this seminar at sea is over, and you get a little experience with the steps, the learning curve will have kicked in, and you will find it pretty simple to know what's coming from the other side."

History Repeats Itself

The group was about to learn that the first indicator of how someone is going to negotiate with you in the future is how they have negotiated with you in the past.

"Many people are just not comfortable or skilled in using more than one of the four negotiation strategies," stated Dr. Pat. "Just like you, they experience negotiaphobia that traps them in their own comfort zone, and additionally, over 99 percent of them have not had this training. If they were competitive with you in the last negotiation, they will most likely play win-lose with you this time around as well. Such is the case even if it did not work out all that well for them. The best predictor of future behavior is past behavior. In cards, bluffers tend to bluff often, and folders tend to be folders. That is how they like to play, even without thinking about it. All you have to do in this assessment of the other side is be observant enough to recognize it."

Dr. Pat went on to share a story that reinforced history repeating itself. "I have a client who has a customer I unaffectionately call Mr. 10 Percent. Every year when they negotiate a new annual contract with this guy, he takes the highly competitive stance of immediately demanding a 10 percent price reduction, regardless of his growing business and accompanying service requirements. Some of my clients think I have a crystal ball that helps me see into the future because I am pretty accurate in my prediction of what other parties are going to say and do at the table. This ability is not based on any peek into the future. It is instead driven by my careful observation and assessment of what has happened in the past."

Jay thoughtfully agreed that most of the times when he was surprised by something his customers said, did, or did not do, he should not have been caught off guard. He had often gone to meetings hoping against hope that he would experience something different this time around because he still did not have a means to counter those buyers who proclaimed a lack of differentiation or the questionable value of XL's offerings. It was like reliving the same bad dream over and over again.

Taking Things Personally

Dr. Pat next moved to the topic of behavioral styles in anticipating how an individual might negotiate with you. "Even if you have never engaged in a formal negotiation with someone, and thus have no history to draw upon, you can still assess them. If you observe their behavioral style tendencies, you will have a solid source of input in terms of what strategy they are most likely to deploy." He went on to describe the four basic interaction styles in terms of their pace of information exchange and their focus on either tasks or relationships.

Analyticals (Slow Pace/Task Focus)

Dr. Pat explained that analytical people are the least emotional when it comes to their negotiation encounters. "When you are involved with a numbers person, recognize that what they really want is no surprises," he said. "It's all about a rational evaluation of the numbers. You should minimize any focus on opinions and feelings. They want the hard data, accurately presented, and the time to study it.

Analyticals are like a dog taking a bone and running under a porch to work it over." Dr. Pat explained that for this reason, you can predict that analyticals will make heavy use of the avoidance negotiation strategy. "They avoid making a decision without adequate data and significant time to process it. They also often strongly resist making decisions and expressing opinions in public forums."

Dr. Pat concluded his coverage of how analyticals negotiate by emphasizing, "You had best make certain that they have all the data you want them to consider before they go under that porch, because when they come out they have already made up their mind. To change their mind after that point would be an indication of the one thing these folks fear most in any negotiation: making a mistake."

Drivers (Fast Pace/Task Focus)

"A lot of people are intimidated by negotiating with drivers, but personally, they are my favorite interaction style to work with," Dr. Pat continued. "The beauty of negotiating with drivers, given their short attention span, unemotional task orientation, and direct nature, is that you generally know exactly where you stand with them. They often come at you with an overtly competitive strategy, but this is just a test. They want to see what you're made of and how prepared and confident you are in terms of the issues being negotiated." He then proposed that if you pass their opening salvo test, there is a very good chance to move into a collaborative encounter with a driver. Eduardo had always found such an opening attack painful and disorienting. He now had a much better idea of what was actually taking place.

Dr. Pat went on, "Once they know you're for real, only then do they decide you are worth the effort and candor it takes to collaborate with you. They don't play a win-win card game with many people, but the ones they do deem worthy of this strategy often end up with a lot of chips. They will have their one big issue in any negotiation, and if you can confidently address that point, they have very limited interest in the other 'minor' aspects of the deal. This big issue is the thorn in their paw, and if you find and remove it, the path to success has few other hurdles. When you find them in a hurry to get something they want done completed, they'll often not be predisposed to beat you up very much on price." He explained that they generally aggressively attack price primarily to check your confidence in the value of your proposal.

"You will need to build credibility with a driver, because the one thing they fear most in any negotiation is failure. Unlike analyticals, they don't mind a few mistakes along the way, but you must recognize that failure is simply not an option for them. Their self-image is totally inconsistent with this outcome."

Dr. Pat next suggested that when it comes to working out the details of a deal, drivers have very little patience for these discussions. "When successful, drivers have a valued analytical on their team. Work with this team member to get the *i*'s dotted and *t*'s crossed, but if the driver is the primary decision maker, do not fail to get him or her back in the room to bless the final deal."

At this point, Jay recalled a recent negotiation where he had tried to work out the details with the driver herself. She ended up totally losing interest in doing business with XL, stating, "You guys are just too much trouble to work with." Jay was wishing he had met the One Minute Negotiator years ago. That piece of advice would have saved several large deals that had gotten away from him. A conversation with Eduardo during the next break showed his friend had experienced that same realization.

Expressives (Fast Pace/Relationship Focus)

Dr. Pat described expressives as the ultimate "wannabe" collaborators. "These people love the idea of collaboration. The only problem with them is that they rarely have the attention span and discipline to follow through with this strategy. They are, at their very core, the dreamers we discussed earlier, as they simply don't have enough focus to be sages. When you capture the attention of an expressive in a negotiation, you had best move rapidly and enthusiastically to get a deal done. They may love you today, but tomorrow they will often not even remember your name.

They have moved on down the road and are now working on some other, more exciting negotiation."

He explained that in his coaching efforts, novice negotiators are frequently offended when expressives lose interest and move to avoidance. "These people are impulsive and sometimes flighty. They generally have so many balls in the air that they can only get themselves to even consider their negotiation with you for a brief moment of time. Your best bet is to understand their goals and visions and respond to them in a stimulating manner in an attempt to secure their commitment."

Dr. Pat emphasized the need to find someone in the expressive's organization to work with to collect the information necessary to understand needs, develop options, create an action plan, and then come back to the expressive for a decision. "You really need for them to designate a point person in their camp for you to work with. You have to get their commitment to come back into the negotiations at the decision point, and that point had better be very soon. In this respect, they are similar to drivers. Don't be afraid to be diligent in pushing an expressive to stick with the process. They need this prodding and ultimately will respect it.

"The number one thing they dislike in negotiations is boredom. Come up with solutions respectful of the expressive's goals, present them in a brief and energized manner, and you might be surprised when they grab them in a nanosecond."

As everybody was taking notes, Eduardo reflected back on a time when he had moved too slowly and had seen a potentially highly collaborative expressive prospect disappear, apparently into a witness protection program, never to be seen again.

Amiables (Slow Pace/Relationship Focus)

Dr. Pat opened the discussion of the final style with a question. "Coming into this workshop, how many of you felt that happy, friendly, and caring amiables were the best of all interaction styles with which to negotiate?" Well over half of the hands in the room went up. "My friends, I hate to tell you this, but you were seriously confused. The problem in negotiating with amiables is that you think they love you, but be advised that they love your competitor, too! Their relationship orientation and tendency to resist conflict at all cost keeps them in a friendly mode. They are not in a hurry to make a decision, because it takes a long time to find out how everybody on their team feels about any change. This makes expressives and drivers absolutely climb the wall. I like the word 'yes,' and I am a big boy who can live with a 'no' and work to see if it can be changed, but a 'maybe' in negotiations will eat you alive."

For this reason, he characterized amiables as the ultimate avoiders. "Unlike analyticals, who are avoiding a decision without adequate data or in front of groups, amiables will postpone making a decision until they are certain of an outcome that will not offend anyone on their team, as well as on the other teams competing for their attention. In their mind, they are hoping that if they wait long enough, the issue in question will solve itself or totally disappear."

Dr. Pat suggested that amiables are also the most likely style to accommodate. "In order to stay away from conflict, they will often accommodate beyond that which is even necessary. It may sound good to have an amiable doing this in a negotiation with you, but they are very big on using complaining and sometimes guilt to try to get these accommodations back in spades later in the game."

Figuring Out First-Timers

It was at this point in the discussion that Monte Beal raised his hand. Dr. Pat nodded at him to get his input. "This is all well and good for people we have a history with," Monte said, "but what about first-time negotiation encounters where there is not any experience to draw on?"

Dr. Pat responded, "Monte, I owe you $5, because that is a great segue for where we are going next. You have two sources of assessment information when you have not negotiated with a person in the past or have no input regarding their behavioral style." The first point identified was the company you are negotiating with, if it is a business-to-business encounter. "The number one thing I want to know when I have not negotiated with people in a company before is, 'How does that organization negotiate with their customers?' If they have a reputation for working collaboratively with their customers, I expect them to be collaborative with their vendors or suppliers. On the other hand, when they face highly competitive encounters with their customers, I fully expect them to be competitive in their dealings with me as I sell to them. These are cultural issues that can give us some valuable predictability."

Dr. Pat also recommended looking at public information on the organization, such as websites and published articles. "If they are openly sharing useful information, that approach is consistent with collaboration. You can also look for words like *cooperation, value, relationships,* and even *collaboration* in their mission and vision statements. Conversely, if they are secretive beyond address and phone number, that assessment signals the selection of a competitive strategy.

"You certainly have to be aware of the inherent differences between public and private organizations with regard to the amount of information they share, but I feel that, with a little effort, you can begin to assess which way the organizational culture leans. You can also talk to people in other noncompetitive organizations who have negotiated with this company in the past to get a read on where they tend to fall on the negotiation strategy matrix. All of these inputs just take a little bit of effort, but the insights are often extremely valuable."

A Parting Warning

"Before we leave this issue and take a break," Dr Pat told the group, "I want to take one minute to plant a final thought in your mind.

"When my assessment of the other side leaves doubts in my mind, I always lean toward anticipating a collaborative encounter. As you will come to see, it takes a bit more planning to negotiate this way, but I can usually readily switch to a competitive strategy if I start out carefully using collaboration. It is much more difficult, and frequently impossible, to make the opposite switch due to the walls that are put in place when my strategizing has me opening competitively. If anyone is going to be responsible for missing what was a collaborative opportunity to generate superior outcomes, I want it to be them and not me. I don't want to have to look in the mirror and admit that by my own lack of preparation and information sharing, a quick move to a position, or a lack of flexibility, I steered this negotiation down the more limited competitive path. I do not want to show all my cards at the start of the conversation, but I will share an overview of where I stand and see what sort of sharing I get back from them in return.

"Now that we have brought the topic into play, we will fully move into the third EASY treatment step of strategizing in the next session."

Jay could tell that this approach was well received by his colleagues in the room as they made their final notes and moved to grab a beverage and a snack.

CHAPTER 6 ONE MINUTE INSIGHTS

1. Our success in negotiating is dependent on our ability to correctly assess the strategies being used by others.
2. Many negotiators are highly predictable because their negotiaphobia leaves them feeling comfortable repeatedly using the same strategy time and again.
3. Knowing the behavioral style of the participants, as well as the culture of their company, can help predict the negotiation strategy they will use with us.
4. When the assessment of the other side leaves doubt, we should strategize to open with a careful collaborative strategy, as it is easier to move from collaboration to competition than vice versa.

CHAPTER 7

Strategizing: One Size Does Not Fit All

Taking Measurements

In the next segment of the workshop, Dr. Patrick Perkins moved to Step 3 of the negotiaphobia treatment process he was prescribing: strategize as you select the proper strategy for this particular negotiation.

"You will recall that one of the symptoms of negotiaphobia is using the same negotiation strategy irrespective of the situation you are facing. Experience has shown me that none of the four strategies that should go through your mind as you review Step 1 of the treatment are *universally* appropriate or inappropriate. As we discussed in the last session, you may be up against a highly competitive driver; and if you try to use collaboration, you are really unintentionally doing what, Jay?"

A bit shocked, Jay responded, "Accommodating without a tourniquet." Dr. Pat smiled and nodded. Jay was glad Dr. Pat liked him. He could not imagine what it would feel like being on the wrong side of this guy.

Dr. Pat continued, "Let's now look at factors we should consider as we quickly scan the situation and strategize to find the optimal fit for a given set of circumstances. For this discussion, keep in mind that Step 3 builds on Step 2, so you will need to consider your personal tendencies, as well as what you have just learned about the most likely strategy to be deployed by the other side."

Your One Minute Drill: Each time you begin a negotiation situation, take a minute to review the three steps.

STEP 3

Strategize: **Select the proper strategy for this particular negotiation.**

STEP 2

Assess: Evaluate your tendency to use each of the negotiation strategies, as well as the tendencies of the other side(s).

STEP 1

Engage: Recognize you are in a negotiation and quickly review the viable strategies.

Both Eduardo and Jay were now very curious as to whether the preliminary decisions they had made about several of their customers and prospects would match the guidance from Dr. Pat's strategizing discussion.

When Does an Ostrich Fly?

Dr. Pat opened the strategizing discussion in the lower left corner of the matrix introduced in Step 1. He indicated that there are some situations when not engaging (avoidance) is the best negotiation strategy. "Avoidance has the potential to be the best strategy for you or others when the topic is a minimal issue, or when a superior option is readily available elsewhere." He then put a caveat on this directive. "The problem with avoiding what at the time may seem to be a minimal issue is that, over time that insignificant issue can grow exponentially in importance. So, where avoidance may look like a good strategy to use today, it may turn out to be an inappropriate fit for negotiations with that same party six months from now."

Demonstrating the homework he had done on XL team members' negotiation challenges, Dr. Pat used the example of a good customer wanting one hour of free technical support. "At a billing rate of $200 an hour, this is not that large an amount for a good five-figure revenue client. It might be tempting to use an avoidance strategy and just do it. When multiplied by 10, however, that number becomes a significant situation with $2,000 on the line. I recommend the use of what I call a 'no-charge invoice' for very good customers when facing a request like this. This is far superior to avoiding the discussion of the additional investment issue, which in this instance would be de facto accommodation. That approach is playing unnecessarily in the bottom half of the strategy matrix.

"The first hour should be invoiced at $200, with 'no charge' in the bottom right 'amount due' box. Send this unique document to them via e-mail, but *do not* submit it to XL's accounts receivable department. If the customer likes the result from the service and then wants ten more hours, they now understand what it's worth, and you should let them know they will now be invoiced for the appropriate total. If we avoid in this situation and just give our services away, they ain't worth a plug nickel." Dr. Pat went on to say the no-charge invoice also demonstrates the investments we have made in the relationship over time much better than a traditional avoidance-or accommodation-based approach. This technique helps make future negotiations much more collaborative.

The second possibility identified where avoidance is a proper strategy is when we or the other side recognize the significance of the issue but feel better served by continuing negotiations with other parties. "When you have a bird in the hand, and you really like that bird, why would you go reaching into another thorny bush in search of a different one?" Dr. Pat reasoned in his Texas drawl. He elaborated that if a sales organization was one of several firms that presented solutions to a prospect, and the negotiators for that prospect have no questions and don't return calls, then their avoidance strategy indicates that this alternative is no longer in the running.

"Salespeople generally despise objections in negotiations, but, in reality, objections are almost always a sign of some interest. No one objects about the time it will take to transition to a new information system if they have absolutely no interest in changing. Likewise, they usually don't push you about your pricing if they already have a favorable option that is significantly more economical. They simply say, 'Thank you, and we will get back to you,' and then send out a 'You were nice, but you lost' e-mail. Given that negotiations consume valuable resources, why would someone continue to negotiate with another party they see as materially inferior to their better alternatives for the situation they face?"

Jay had to agree with Dr. Pat that avoidance was the most painful and frustrating strategy from the other side he had ever experienced in his career. He also thought of the many times he had used this very strategy as a sign of disinterest with colleagues, and he even had to admit to utilizing avoidance with Laura on the house and other issues. Earlier this month she had sent him a text asking for dates he would be available to meet with a real estate agent she met and liked. He simply did not respond, hoping he could claim the "lost in cyberspace" excuse should she ever bring it up.

When to Bleed

Next, Dr. Pat positioned accommodation as an appropriate strategy for situations when we are in a significantly weaker leverage position that is obvious to all sides and have no other options with which to negotiate. He indicated that understanding leverage is essential when strategizing about the need to accommodate. Dr. Pat clarified this key negotiation term by stating, "Leverage is the ability of one side to influence what another side thinks, says, or does. It can be generated by a party's ability to reward or punish us. We are in a much weaker power position in comparison to the tow truck driver who can severely punish us by simply driving off if we attempt to negotiate the price per gallon to get fuel in our empty gas tank in the middle of the desert. An improper scan of the power situation as you strategize will leave you scanning the sky above for buzzards." Everybody snickered at the Texan's analogy.

According to Dr. Pat, another important source of power today is knowledge leverage. This comes from our information analysis and preparation in understanding the situation, and the development of insights into how to make all sides more successful. The least prepared or knowledgeable side of the negotiation table is frequently the one feeling the need or being pushed to accommodate. Jay made another note to himself that gaining knowledge leverage would be critical in moving out of what had been an accommodation strategy with MGB Properties, and perhaps others.

Dr. Pat next emphasized that *how* we accommodate as our strategizing leads us in this direction is just as important as knowing *when* to do it. He clarified that the subservient comment should be carefully phrased and rehearsed. He recommended it be something on the order of "This time around, due to the unique situation we find ourselves in, we would be willing to entertain what you propose be done to address the issues of concern, and reach an agreement." The "this time around" comment was stressed by Dr. Pat as a critical component of the statement, because a proficient negotiator wants to avoid setting a negative precedent for ongoing accommodation.

"Let me also stress that you should indicate you are only willing to *entertain* the other side's proposal, but not automatically agree to it. It only takes a little

90

bit of effort to carefully craft this comment, and days, weeks, or even years to deal with the consequences when it is poorly phrased or not voiced at all."

According to Dr. Pat, "An interesting aspect of accommodation with other parties is that when you do it properly, the other side will frequently ask for less than you were willing to give up to rectify mistakes that have been made. Here you may be willing to give them the entire cow, but they only want a couple of T-bones." He explained that he had worked with one group that had received $75,000 to conduct a project that, for a variety of reasons, including team member turnover, had not even been started several months after the contract was signed and the check deposited. "Having taken a minute with me to strategize, they appropriately went to the meeting in an accommodation mind-set, willing to return the money in full to their client. After using the phrasing suggested here, the customer responded, 'Just go ahead and do the darn project. I wanted it done, and I still do. If I had wanted the money, I would have kept it in the first place.'"

Dr. Pat went on to explain that when we find ourselves in a situation calling for accommodation, we should not go into a laundry list of excuses. The other side almost never cares about why we failed to perform and instead is primarily interested in us taking ownership and suggesting going-forward solutions.

Times to Battle

Moving to the top half of the matrix, strategizing resulting in the use of a competitive strategy, Dr. Pat said this approach is appropriate when we have a negotiation involving an opponent not inclined to or capable of collaborating, or one simply not worth the effort. The lack of capability may come from our lack of success in getting senior-level decision makers in the room or be due to a general lack of collaborative skills on their side.

"I often hear people say they have a collaborative relationship with a lower-level purchasing agent or salesperson. This is rarely possible. To have a situation that fosters collaboration, you need the senior players in the loop because they are the ones most likely to know their side's true needs and can communicate such. These members of top management can then provide input regarding alternatives and make decisions about the options we propose, as well as secure funding and other resources. As you strategize, you need to look for these pieces of the puzzle if you decide to collaborate; and if some are missing, and you have some leverage, competition would frequently be your best option."

The not-worth-the-effort aspect of strategizing calling for a competitive approach generated some discussion among the participants. Dr. Pat strongly emphasized the need to look beyond the current negotiation encounter to the true *potential* afforded by the encounter. "Many car dealers negotiate with you in a highly competitive fashion because they fully expect to never see you again. The exception would be organizations like Carl Sewell in Texas. Carl's book, *Customers for Life,* outlines Sewell's strategy for taking a longer-term and more collaborative approach to working with their customers in meeting their and their family's transportation needs."

Dr. Pat continued with his clarification of situation potential by stressing that some customers will negotiate a small piece of business with a new vendor just to experience their approach and capabilities. They are giving the new resource the opportunity, with a strong collaborative performance, to earn additional and more substantial business. He stated that when strategizing, it is usually better to err on the side of thinking that there could be more potential than underestimating the opportunity.

When to Win-Win, and Win Again

The Step 3 strategizing segment of the workshop was concluded by clarifying the circumstances when a particular negotiation guides us toward a collaborative approach.

"You want to at least try to collaborate when the situation presents a significant opportunity with capable and willing decision-making teams on all sides of the table," Dr. Pat advised. "Most people call collaboration a win-win strategy, but I have found it instructive to add in a third win. When we successfully collaborate, you win, I win, and, perhaps most importantly, the relationship between us or our companies wins as we gain a much broader and deeper understanding of each other's capabilities and needs. I regularly see cases of two companies doing business with each other for forty years, with the players in each changing several times. The relationship itself is vitally important." Dr. Pat indicated that his strategizing experience has shown that two sides being willing and able to collaborate only happens in about one in five of all the negotiations most people engage in. Bringing in Pareto's law, commonly known as the 80/20 rule, he went on to say that this relatively small percentage of all negotiations normally represents about 80 percent of most people's and organizations' overall success.

He continued, "The time and effort it takes to collaborate requires that we reserve the selection of this strategy for a very special set of negotiations. The amount of preparation and need identification necessary to foster a problem-solving environment is only justified due to the superior and long-lasting outcomes that can be achieved when our strategizing shows this fourth strategy is appropriate and then is successfully utilized. The candor required to collaborate must be based on a high level of trust and a low level of interpersonal stress. Everyone must feel that the information being shared between parties will be authentic and used for the common good, not for opportunistic ploys to achieve personal gains."

Dr. Pat proposed that participants should always seek to select a collaborative strategy for negotiations between different parties within the XL organization. "Internal negotiations can be extremely difficult at times due to conflicting goals and objectives. However, when marketing, sales, production, finance, and research and development can pull together using a collaborative approach, there are few limitations in terms of what this organization can accomplish. That said, our strategizing frequently shows we are fighting for the same 'pork chop' when it comes to organizational resources."

Eduardo and Jay gave each other that knowing look indicating that XL had a long way to go to get to the point where most of the internal negotiations could be collaborative rather than competitive turf battles.

Setting Up the Drill

Dr. Pat concluded the session by indicating that they would next be moving into the Y of the EASY process. "Your One Minute Drill is a process you engage in each time you face a negotiation situation. You will simply take a minute to review the three steps that comprise the negotiaphobia treatment process. You should recall that we started with Step 1, Engage, where you recognize that a negotiation is necessary and review the four negotiation strategies. Then we moved to Step 2—Assess your own strategy tendencies and the likely strategies to be deployed by the other side. Finally, in Step 3, you identify the strategy that fits the situation. By reviewing these three steps, you are conducting your drill to succeed in any negotiation you might face. With only limited practice, this should be a drill you can complete in only one very valuable minute."

Eduardo was looking forward to using this drill. He was expecting that Anderson Industries had the potential and could be worth the effort of investing in a full collaborative strategy. He made a note on his action items list to complete his drill again to see if it supported collaborating with this client upon his return to Florida. He had already made notes of customers that seemed to match the other three strategies in terms of their potential and how he believed they negotiate with him. His use of the One Minute Drill would help him clarify the strategic path he would at least initially follow for each of these negotiations.

At the same time, Jay was wondering about the use of a competitive approach at MGB Properties. He had never been able to get the organization's senior players engaged in discussions about information system needs or solutions. The use of a competitive strategy was looking like his best alternative.

CHAPTER 7 ONE MINUTE INSIGHTS

1. Skilled strategizing will show there is a time and place for selecting the avoidance and accommodation strategies, despite the generally inferior outcomes they tend to generate.

2. Although people don't like objections in a negoti-ation, they are better than the deadening silence one encounters when facing an avoider.

3. A competitive strategy is often the best one to select when our strategizing shows this is an in-significant deal, but we must be careful not to judge the significance of a deal only by its cover.

4. Collaboration requires a great deal more work than the other three strategies, but when our strategizing leads us in this direction, the returns can make it more than worth this investment.

CHAPTER 8

Your One Minute Drill in Practice

Drilling for Black Gold

"Jay, do you really think we can review the three steps in the negotiaphobia treatment in a drill that just takes one minute and end up with the negotiation strategy that gives the best chance for success?" Eduardo asked.

"Well, Eduardo, the ideas Dr. Pat has come up with are pretty simple and straightforward," Jay replied. "I like the EASY approach of engage, assess, strategize. I have already developed some ideas about how to change my negotiation strategies with several clients and prospects. What about Anderson Industries for you? Much of the time he was talking about collaboration, I was thinking about how you always thought there was so much opportunity over there. Didn't you tell me a couple of weeks ago they got a new CFO and were headed into an aggressive expansion into Europe? Seems like win-win-win time to me." Eduardo smiled and confirmed his friend's assessment of what could become his most important client.

At that point, Dr. Pat was up in front of the room. "We have a nickname for oil down in my home state of Texas. We call that stuff 'black gold' 'cause it is so valuable. It can be tough to find, too. It is usually thousands of feet down, and you often have to drill for months to find it. If you don't hit it, you end up with some of the deepest post holes you'll ever see.

"The drill we have been building here makes it much easier to find your own version of black gold: proficient negotiations that generate the most favorable outcomes possible, while using up a minimal amount of resources. It is a powerful force to help you fight negotiaphobia and build stronger relationships, where relationships are indeed feasible. The good news is you won't have to drill for weeks or months, but only one minute once you have used your drill just a few times."

Your One Minute Drill: **Each time you begin a negotiation situation, take a minute to review the three steps.**

STEP 3

Strategize: Select the proper strategy for this particular negotiation.

STEP 2

Assess: Evaluate your tendency to use each of the negotiation strategies, as well as the tendencies of the other side(s).

STEP 1

Engage: Recognize you are in a negotiation and quickly review the viable strategies.

Dr. Pat proceeded to give them the three questions that comprise the One Minute Drill:

1. Is this situation a negotiation; and if so, what are the four viable negotiation strategies?
2. What are my natural negotiation strategy tendencies; and for the other parties in this negotiation, what strategy are they most likely to deploy?
3. Recognizing the nature of this particular negotiation situation, what is the optimal strategy to use?

He then walked the group through several of his examples, as well as working through several examples put forth by XL team members.

With that done, it was time for the group to spend the final evening of the cruise celebrating with their loved ones and the next day return home to become proficient One Minute negotiators.

Time Flies: Four Months Later

Jay and Eduardo had been successfully using their One Minute Drill ever since the ship had docked back in Miami. They both had learned that, in both their personal and professional lives, the drill for treating their negotiaphobia was producing barrels of "oil." Dr. Pat had cautioned all the participants at the end of the workshop that no process can make someone a winner in each and every negotiation, and their newfound drill was no exception. He did share his belief that we learn as much or more from our defeats as from our victories. His point that "the goal of the One Minute Drill composed of three simple questions is always to decrease the first percentage and grow the second one" had proven profound.

Reflecting on Their Negotiations

As schedules had worked out, Dr. Pat was in Miami at the same time Jay and Laura had flown down from Cleveland to look at potential investment/vacation homes in Key Largo with Eduardo and Luciana. They had arranged a time to get together with Dr. Pat at a restaurant to discuss how the One Minute Drill was working so far. It was a wonderful opportunity for the two of them to share their results with their mentor and gain some additional insights on how to use it more effectively.

"Jay, why don't we start with you?" Dr. Pat said. "I believe you came to realize that the drill is as powerful in your personal life as in your business negotiations. Give me an example of where you have found the drill helped you negotiate with your friends or family."

"Well, Dr. Pat," Jay replied, "I have to say that the drill has had some very meaningful impacts. Before the cruise, my sister had approached me about a health issue with our father. She was concerned that his general forgetfulness was turning into something more. Her concern was that he was in the early stages of Alzheimer's disease. I thought there was nothing going on that was particularly unusual for a guy his age. Prior to the workshop, I did not see this as a negotiation, only the views of an overcautious sibling. Given this mind-set, there was no move to engage Step 1 of recognizing the situation and reviewing the strategies.

"Upon my return to Cleveland, a quick review of my tendencies in Step 2 showed me that I was really avoiding this issue. To my sister's credit, she was looking to collaborate with me on it. Moving into review of Step 3, I realized that given the significance of my father's health and well-being, and the willingness of my sister to work with me, it was clear that collaboration was the best option—and really the only option.

"The big value from my One Minute Drill was to help me put it all in perspective and recognize this as a true and significant negotiation. I met my sister for lunch, and we laid out a plan where she would do the first round of information collection, and then we would both meet with Dad's doctor and come up with an action plan. The bad news is he has been diagnosed as having this disease; the good news is he is getting proper treatment, and our collaboration has led to some options that all of us feel good about."

Dr. Pat was clearly pleased with this application of the drill. "Jay, thank you for sharing that personal experience. I have to tell you that while the primary focus of the workshops I do is on business applications, the personal applications are the ones I get the greatest satisfaction from. We often don't even recognize the negotiations that crop up in our lives, and thus we default to an avoidance strategy that is frequently inappropriate, and often even dangerous. If we don't review and engage Step 1, it is highly unlikely that we will end up with such a positive outcome."

He turned to Eduardo. "Eduardo, what about an XL application of the drill from you, where you used it with a client or prospect?"

Eduardo could hardly wait to share his story from Anderson Industries. "Dr. Pat, much of the time we were going through the workshop, I was thinking about Anderson Industries. They have been a good client of XL for many years, but I have become concerned over the past six months that they were changing so much that the information system we were providing them had become obsolete. It was tempting to not engage and just sit back and see if anything bad happened—you know, don't rock the boat. After my time with you, I knew this was not the best approach. My use of the drill clarified for me that it was time to take Anderson to a new level.

"After the cruise, I reviewed Step 1. The first call I made was to my day-to-day contact there. I learned that Anderson had hired a woman to be their new CFO. I had not yet met with her. As a matter of fact, there had been almost no contact between XL and the prior CFO. I told the system manager that it was time for us to get together with her and discuss all the changes that were taking place at Anderson. He reluctantly agreed, which takes me to the review of Step 2. His name is Gary, and he tends to be an avoider. Gary's motto has been to stay under the radar screen of top management. My tendency has simply been to accommodate and see if we could make minor changes, essentially Band-aids, without pushing Gary for a larger investment in this critical part of their operations. I did some homework on the new CFO and learned that while she is a driver, make no mistake about that, she was very involved in a collaborative effort with XL at her prior company. Moving to a review of Step 3, I decided that given the significance of the opportunity and the ability to get her in the room, we had to at least attempt a collaborative approach."

Dr. Pat chimed in, "How has that worked out for you?"

Eduardo continued, "Well, through the use of my One Minute Drill, it was apparent that while she came out with a competitive stance of tight budgetary constraints, with several questions I was able to get her to share that Anderson Industries had aggressive plans for expansion into Eastern Europe. This was to be done via a joint venture partner in Budapest. After bringing in our technical people and getting them to do an assessment, we found several major gaps in the ability of the present Anderson system to support this move. It was a big help when we discovered that one of their competitors with a system from one of our competitors was involved in a multimillion-dollar data security breach judgment. After several weeks of work, the XL team I assembled went back to Gary and the new CFO with two options to put in place a system that would meet their needs not only today but into the future. After some discussions around scope of service and price, they decided to move forward with the most aggressive option. We are going to be implementing that deliverable over the next several weeks. Without the drill, I would still be using my combination of avoidance, accommodation, and hope!"

Dr. Pat was again thrilled that the application of the drill had produced such positive results. "Eduardo, as I shared with you, one of the symptoms of negotiaphobia is continuing to simply live with an inadequate solution. In the fast-paced world we live in today, just because a system was a good choice two years ago, does not mean it will work today. You now recognize the rewards of engaging the process with a review of Step 1 in the drill. At the very worst, you would have ended up validating that your present solution was still working, but you ended up with something that is far superior for both Anderson and XL."

Looking at Jay, he asked, "Jay, what about the use of the drill at XL for you?"

Jay was clearly not as excited as Eduardo about this stage of their conversation. "Well, Dr. Pat, you said it does not always lead to success, and I am living proof. The customer I couldn't get off my mind during the workshop is MGB Properties. When you talked about the types of people and organizations that use a competitive strategy, it was like you were specifically describing them. They pride themselves on using their procurement department to beat up 'vendors'—and they do not use that word as a term of endearment. This group's role is to shake the trees every few months and then rake up all the money that falls out. We had accommodated and accommodated with them over the last two years to the point that not only was XL not making any money, but MGB's system had not kept pace and was becoming dysfunctional for their users. I hate to admit it, but we had a lose-lose situation going on."

Dr. Pat was now very curious to see how things played out. "Jay, tell us how your One Minute Drill worked for you with MGB."

"I have to admit that MGB began the negotiation by sending me an e-mail from procurement asking for accommodation. The word they used was their desire for us to 'partner' with them by dropping our prices another 5 percent, so the Step 1 engagement review was in play right out of the gate. I knew I was in a negotiation situation and was considering the strategy options. My move to review Step 2 clearly showed me that I had been trying to collaborate while they had been competitive. I know, Dr. Pat—bleeding without a tourniquet. Moving into review of Step 3, I went to Cathy, my new sales manager, whom you know well; and after an analysis of our profitability from MGB, she said that no way would we continue to accommodate. Our president, Bob Blankenship, backed her up. We all decided we already had the worst-case scenario, and if a change meant them going with someone else, so be it." The understanding of Dr. Patrick Perkins's negotiation principles and the EASY formula with the One Minute Drill had already enabled Jay to transition from a negotiaphobe to an informed practitioner of the drill.

Jay went on to explain that he tried to get MGB's system users and senior management into the room for a needs discovery meeting. Procurement blocked this move, so there was no choice but to go forward with a competitive strategy. He and Cathy came up with two options to put on the table. One was the system that MGB really needed, as best as could be determined under the constrained circumstances. The other was a minor price reduction, but with a significant reduction in the scope of services, and a pay-as-you-go menu for anything beyond the bare-bones system. Both of these options were rejected. MGB went out to a request for proposals, from which they selected the lowest-cost provider with a very negative reputation for user satisfaction.

Dr. Pat now chimed in. "Jay, as you correctly recall, no process can result in success 100 percent of the time, and the fact that you have stopped the bleeding at MGB and sent a message to them and the marketplace does not make this phase of the negotiation a total failure."

Jay was in total agreement. "At MGB we were also reminded that your definition of negotiations clearly indicates that they are an ongoing process. It is very preliminary in nature, but Cathy received some feedback at a social function this past week that the users at MGB are in a revolt over the decision that was made. They have gone directly to upper management with their concerns that information systems are being purchased the same way they buy paper towels. My game plan has been to maintain as much contact with XL's supporters there as we can, and see if their involvement drives a revision of the Step 3 strategy decision. We will not go back in there with a competitive strategy, but we are still open to a true collaboration; however, it takes both sides. As you told us, Dr. Pat, in negotiations, 'no' simply means 'not yes yet.'"

Dr. Pat was very pleased that Jay had remembered this comment. Jay went on to share that the resources that were being squandered on MGB Properties are now being allocated to two very promising prospects, one of whom showed immediate interest upon being contacted. "I ran them through my One Minute Drill: Is it a negotiation, and what are the strategy options? What are my tendencies and those of the other side? And what strategy is a fit in this situation? It became apparent early on that they were excellent candidates for collaboration. Jennifer Harris, our top system development specialist, and I met with them last week, and their VP told us, 'You guys have the best and most comprehensive approach we've seen, and we have more at stake than ever before with our technology platform. I am open to setting up an in-depth discovery meeting so that we can look deeper into our needs and your capabilities.'

"A major component for the success to this point is the way that all the functional areas of XL have pulled together in a collaborative fashion," Jay continued. "While historically the internal discussions had always started out with 'What's my slice?' now most of the time the mind-set is to make a larger pie and bake it properly. We need to have collaboration within the XL team to generate collaboration with our clients. There is really no other way to do it."

Dr. Pat commented about what he had just heard. "One of the greatest benefits of treating your negotiaphobia through the One Minute Drill is that you start making more intelligent decisions about where to put your time and effort. Your use of the process with MGB shows one of the major benefits from this process. There are many good collaborative opportunities out there, even in challenging times. The key is not to let the highly competitive negotiations consume and blind you. You are absolutely correct about the internal/external collaboration chain. Both links must be in place to make it happen."

The next round of beverages was on Dr. Pat, as they continued discussing how the One Minute Drill was becoming second nature for them and was significantly impacting all areas of their lives.

CHAPTER 8 ONE MINUTE INSIGHTS

1. Proficient negotiators reap the rewards of their efforts; solid strategies generate superior outcomes. It's as EASY as 1, 2, 3.
2. If we ever stop treating our negotiaphobia and developing our skills, we will revert to old habits. As Zig Ziglar says, "Bad habits are easy

to develop and hard to get rid of. Good habits are hard to develop but easy to live with."

3. Internal collaboration is a prerequisite for collaborating with prospects and clients.

4. Negotiations only become EASY when we fully utilize the One Minute Drill. Never quit using it, and it will get easier every time. You will finally be able to unlock the chains of negotiaphobia.

Epilogue: One Year Later

Jay's continued coaching via telephone conversations with Dr. Pat had made him a truly proficient negotiator. Just as valuable as the negotiation skills he learned was his newfound commitment to continue studying his craft. With his coach's guidance, he was even able to get the powers that be at MGB into a collaborative posture, resulting in one of the biggest installations in XL history.

Other prospects were being advanced in more productive directions with his and his team's ongoing use of the One Minute Drill. Jay and Cathy had turned what was a competitive beginning into an amenable working relationship, and then a highly collaborative one. Jay had even come to realize that she and he were in the correct positions at XL. While Jay liked Cathy's title of regional sales manager, he found that there were many aspects of her job that were not so attractive to him. One of which, as Dr. Pat pointed out to him, was having her performance and income being determined by "knuckleheads" like him.

Jay's application of his new skills was instrumental in his winning the golden trophy as top sales professional at XL. Eduardo came in a close second behind Jay in sales performance for the new year, and he vowed to work even harder to beat Jay out of that golden trophy the next time around. Jay told him to always remember that successful negotiations are "EASY," but beating him will not be.

Jay's dad was doing reasonably well, thanks to the timely attention Jay and his sister had paid to his health. Their collaborative relationship had worked very well once Jay had the courage to take a step back, run it through his One Minute Drill, and realize that he had been part of the problem rather than part of the solution.

Jay and Laura had just completed a fairly major renovation and expansion of their home. Jay had shared the drill with her; after agreeing to collaborate based on needs and not emotions, and looking at several options, they decided that they loved their present location. Jay had found many opportunities to use his newfound negotiation skills with the contractor they selected.

The One Minute Drill was changing the course of the lives of those who had heard and heeded the One Minute Negotiator's words on the cruise. It was hard to believe that the guy from west Texas in the shiny cowboy boots could have had such an impact!

The One Minute Negotiator Handy Glossary

Accommodation A negotiation strategy based on carefully meeting the demands of the other party due to one's own weaker power position (high cooperation/reactive).

Activation One's tendency to be either proactive or reactive in the engagement process.

Analytical An interaction style that is slow paced and task focused. People who have this style as dominant tend to pursue a negotiation strategy based on data collection and, frequently an avoidance of a decision in public.

Amiable An interaction style that is slow paced and people focused. People with this style as dominant tend to use an accommodation negotiation strategy as they attempt to make everyone happy.

Avoidance A negotiation strategy based on not discussing negotiation issues in the hope that they will somehow get better or simply go away (low co-operation/reactive).

Bargaining Chip Issues Factors in a negotiation that are not particularly important for the side in question.

A negotiator can make concessions on these issues without significant consequences. Movement on bargaining chip issues should take place in order to get assistance with blue chip issues. Note that it should never be implied that such chips are throw away or give away factors.

Blue Chip Issues Aspects of a negotiation that are very important to the side in question. While a person can make concessions on these issues, such a movement will adversely impact the outcome from any negotiated agreement for them.

Collaboration The most advanced of all the negotiation strategies, based on learning all parties' needs to craft a win-win-win outcome (high cooperation/proactive).

Competition A negotiation strategy focused on getting one's own needs and positions addressed. It is a fixed-sum game/win-lose approach where the only way you can get something is for the other party to give something up (low cooperation/proactive).

Compromise A negotiation tactic based on seeking an agreement by splitting the difference between two parties' positions. It should only be used late in a negotiation, with a small gap in positions, over a single issue, where the offer is tied to an immediate agreement.

Concession A reduction in one's own position on any negotiation issue in an effort to close the gap between the position levels of the various parties. It should only be given if something is received in return. A unilateral concession is, in reality, an accommodation.

Cooperation A willingness to work with the other party in an effort to reach an agreement that includes a consideration of that other party's needs.

Countering tactics Defensive competitive negotiation tactics designed to mitigate the impact of offensive tactics by the other side. These tactics are deployed in a reactive fashion to minimize any concessions that must be made as a result of the other side's offensive tactic.

Defensive tactics Tactics that are used to protect one's positions and minimize concessions in a competitive negotiation.

Discovery meeting A session in a collaborative negotiation focused on getting the needs of all sides on the table. Positions and solution proposals should not be discussed in such a meeting.

Driver An interaction style that is fast paced and task focused. People who have this style as dominant tend to pursue a negotiation strategy based on competition to start, but they can be motivated to collaborate if they find it is in their best interests to do so.

Expressive An interaction style that is fast paced and people focused. Individuals who have this style as dominant tend to pursue a negotiation strategy based on collaboration.

Fortifying tactics Competitive negotiation tactics that are deployed proactively to protect positions and reduce the need to make concessions.

Negotiaphobia A widespread fear of negotiating caused by two things: a desire to avoid conflict, and a lack of skill; the symptoms are manifested two ways: one is the failure to recognize negotiation opportunities, and the other is the inability to adjust one's negotiation strategy to match the situation at hand. We call the individuals suffering from this epidemic *negotiaphobes.*

Negotiation The ongoing process through which two or more parties, whose initial positions are not necessarily consistent, work in an effort to reach an agreement.

Non-negotiables Issues in a negotiation where movement is not possible. These issues should be few in number and clearly stated as not open to negotiation. From that point a negotiator should demonstrate no willingness to even discuss these issues.

Offensive tactics Actions taken by a negotiator in a competitive negotiation that are designed to stimulate accommodations or concessions from the other side.

Opening Ceremonies The start of the meeting that sets the tone for a collaborative or competitive approach. It ends with the introduction of the agenda.

Problem-solving environment An approach to information sharing between parties to a negotiation that puts the emphasis on disclosing and meeting needs with solutions that are jointly developed.

Relational Objectives Outcomes that one is seeking in a negotiation that advance the process of collaboration between the parties. Such objectives are not appropriate for a purely competitive meeting.

Solution Meeting A negotiation session that focuses on confirming needs, identifying the ability of the present solution to meet those needs, introduces new options, discussing those options, and then laying out an action plan going forward.

Transactional Objectives Outcomes that one is seeking to advance the quality of the deal that is presently being negotiated. These targets are more short-term in nature than relational objectives, and are appropriate for use with all negotiation strategies.

Acknowledgments

For both of us, this book is a culmination of years of study, research, practical application, and testing. We have learned much from many, as is the case with most topical areas of subject matter. The in-the-field applications of our concepts with client firms that helped us refine and simplify our model have been informative and gratifying. We appreciate and value, too, the works on negotiations by those who have preceded us, including Gary Frasier, Chester Karras, Roger Dawson, Dr. Jim Hennig, Bob Gibson, John P. Dolan, William Ury, and Roger Fisher.

We cannot say enough about the expertise and effort of Steve Piersanti, who, with the title of publisher of Berrett-Koehler, has demonstrated his executive acumen beyond question, but who many of us know is one of the most skilled editors in the business. We further acknowledge and thank Stephen Caldwell, Sharon Dismore, and Ruth Ann Hensley for their able assistance in the editing of the book.

We also wish to acknowledge the influence of Dr. Ken Blanchard, with whom Don coauthored *The One Minute Entrepreneur.* He not only wrote a very nice foreword for us but also set a terrific example for all of us of how business should be done today, as evidenced by the global success of the Ken Blanchard Companies.

We thank and acknowledge Don's fellow Speakers Roundtable member, Dr. Tony Alessandra, with whom

120

Don coauthored *Selling with Style,* for his early research on behavioral styles and adaptability that are included in this work. We further thank the early researchers/experts on behavioral styles, including Dr. Carl Jung, Dr. David Merrill, Roger Reid, Larry Wilson, and Don Thoren.

Acknowledgement is also in order for Dr. Patrick L. Schul, who pioneered, along with George, some of the early elements of the collaboration concepts that ultimately influenced the subject matter of this book.

About the Authors

Don Hutson

Don Hutson's career spanning speaking, writing, consulting, and sales has brought him many honors. He worked his way through the University of Memphis, graduating with a degree in sales. After a successful sales career, he established his own training firm and today is CEO of U.S. Learning based in Memphis, Tennessee.

Photo Credit: Charles Bush

He has spoken for over two-thirds of the Fortune 500, is featured in over a hundred training films, and currently addresses some seventy-five audiences per year. He is the author or coauthor of twelve books, including the number one *Wall Street Journal* and *New York Times* best-seller, *The One Minute Entrepreneur* (with Ken Blanchard).

His first book, *The Sale,* is in its ninth printing and has been adopted as the sales training primer by dozens of corporations. Don's knowledge and platform expertise in selling value rather than price have been sought out by companies all over the free world. To date, he has addressed over five thousand audiences in twenty-two countries.

Don was on the original board and is a past president of the Society of Entrepreneurs. He is a recipient of the Marguerite Piazza/St. Jude Children's Hospital Humanitarian Award. He serves on the advisory board of *Success* magazine and is chairman of the board of Executive Books.

He was on the founding board of the National Speakers Association and is a past president. He is a member of the prestigious Speakers Roundtable, a think tank of twenty of America's top speakers/trainers. He is a recipient of the Cavett Award, as NSA's member of the year, and is a member of the Speakers Hall of Fame.

To contact Don, call (901)767-5700 or visit www.DonHutson.com.

George Lucas

For over twenty-five years, George Lucas, PhD, has been a resource to organizations as a speaker, trainer, consultant, and field coach. He has worked closely with his clients to assist them in the advancement of best practices as they work to build profitable relationships with their clients, prospects, vendors, and internal resources. George has conducted these initiatives across North America, Asia/Pacific, Europe, Latin America, and Africa.

Photo Credit: Woody Woodliff

124

His client list includes both global and midsize organizations. Of note is that none of his clients has a strategy of being the "cheapest" option in providing services and products to their clients. They all, however, have developed an approach centered on identifying, delivering, communicating, and being compensated appropriately for the value they provide.

Lucas received his bachelor's degree from the University of Missouri–Columbia and subsequently served in several field sales positions. He returned to Missouri to complete both an MBA and PhD in business administration. George has held faculty positions at both Texas A&M University and the University of Memphis. It was at the University of Memphis that he collaborated with Dr. Patrick Schul on the development and delivery of the first graduate-level negotiation skills curriculum.

George is the author of several successful books and has published numerous articles on the topics of negotiation skills, leadership, and marketing strategy. He is Executive Vice President and on the board of U.S. Learning. With Terri Murphy, he coauthored a widely utilized CD-based learning resource entitled *Negotiation: What You Don't Know Can Cost You.*

To contact George, call (901) 767-5700 or visit www.oneminutenegotiator.com

THE AUTHORS' SERVICES

Don Hutson and George Lucas have a collective 65 years of experience in training and educating sales, management, and procurement professionals. U.S. Learning is the organization through which they coordinate all speaking, training, and educational activities. The deliverables vary by client need, but include speech and seminar appearances at corporate and association conventions; tailored training programs from half-day to full week taught on-site at client facilities; coaching client teams on specific significant negotiations; video and e-based training; corporate retreats; and developing distinctive selling strategies and the tools to support their successful execution.

All deliverables are based on in-depth client needs analysis and are tailored to the specific objectives and training needs agreed upon. The topical areas Hutson and Lucas most frequently cover are:

Negotiations Principles
Negotiation Strategies
Selling Value
Marketing Strategies
Entrepreneurship
High Performance Selling
Leadership
Customer Loyalty
Personal Planning and Career Development

For an initial conversation or to set up an in-depth discovery meeting with Don and/or George call 800-647-9166 in Memphis, Tennessee (central time zone). They have created successful programs for hundreds of organizations, in dozens of industries, on six continents, and would be pleased to discuss your needs and help you identify the optimal resources to help you achieve your goals and objectives. Also, we welcome you to visit www.DonHutson.com or www.USLearning.com for more information.

⬤ Berrett–Koehler
̄B̄K̄ Publishers

Berrett-Koehler is an independent publisher dedicated to an ambitious mission: *Creating a World That Works for All.*

We believe that to truly create a better world, action is needed at all levels—individual, organizational, and societal. At the individual level, our publications help people align their lives with their values and with their aspirations for a better world. At the organizational level, our publications promote progressive leadership and management practices, socially responsible approaches to business, and humane and effective organizations. At the societal level, our publications advance social and economic justice, shared prosperity, sustainability, and new solutions to national and global issues.

A major theme of our publications is "Opening Up New Space." Berrett-Koehler titles challenge conventional thinking, introduce new ideas, and foster positive change. Their common quest is changing the underlying beliefs, mindsets, institutions, and structures that keep generating the same cycles of problems, no matter who our leaders are or what improvement programs we adopt.

We strive to practice what we preach—to operate our publishing company in line with the ideas in our books. At the core of our approach is stewardship, which we define as a deep sense of responsibility to administer the company for the benefit of all of our "stakeholder" groups: authors, customers, employees, investors, service providers, and the communities and environment around us.

We are grateful to the thousands of readers, authors, and other friends of the company who consider themselves to be part of the "BK Community." We hope that you, too, will join us in our mission.

A BK Business Book

This book is part of our BK Business series. BK Business titles pioneer new and progressive leadership and management practices in all types of public, private, and nonprofit organizations. They promote socially responsible approaches to business, innovative organizational change methods, and more humane and effective organizations.

Berrett–Koehler Publishers

A community dedicated to creating
a world that works for all

Visit Our Website: www.bkconnection.com
Read book excerpts, see author videos and Internet movies, read our authors' blogs, join discussion groups, download book apps, find out about the BK Affiliate Network, browse subject-area libraries of books, get special discounts, and more!

Subscribe to Our Free E-Newsletter, the BK Communiqué

Be the first to hear about new publications, special discount offers, exclusive articles, news about bestsellers, and more! Get on the list for our free e-newsletter by going to www.bkconnection.com.

Get Quantity Discounts

Berrett-Koehler books are available at quantity discounts for orders of ten or more copies. Please call us toll-free at (800) 929-2929 or email us at bkp.orders@aidcvt.com.

Join the BK Community

BKcommunity.com is a virtual meeting place where people from around the world can engage with kindred spirits to create a world that works for all. BKcommunity.com members may create their own profiles, blog, start and participate in forums and discussion groups, post photos and videos, answer surveys, announce and register for upcoming events, and chat with others online in real time. Please join the conversation!

Books For ALL Kinds of Readers

At ReadHowYouWant we understand that one size does not fit all types of readers. Our innovative, patent pending technology allows us to design new formats to make reading easier and more enjoyable for you. This helps improve your speed of reading and your comprehension. Our EasyRead printed books have been optimized to improve word recognition, ease eye tracking by adjusting word and line spacing as well as minimizing hyphenation. Our EasyRead SuperLarge editions have been developed to make reading easier and more accessible for vision-impaired readers. We offer Braille and DAISY formats of our books and all popular E-Book formats.

We are continually introducing new formats based upon research and reader preferences. Visit our web-site to see all of our formats and learn how you can Personalize our books for yourself or as gifts. Sign up to Become A RHYW Registered Reader.

www.readhowyouwant.com

Made in the USA
Columbia, SC
24 March 2020